The Memoir
of a White House Dog

My Life with President Franklin Roosevelt.

1940-1945

Barbara Guerriero-Flites

Contents

Acknowledgments...7

Introduction..9

Chapter 1 11
Introduction and a Hot Dog Picnic - August 8, 1940 11

Chapter 2 15
Springwood at Hyde Park - November 30, 1940 15

Chapter 3 19
Polio - November 28, 1940..19

Chapter 4 23
Hyde Park, and New York City, New York - December 3, 1940.........23

Chapter 5 31
Washington, D.C. and The White House - November 17, 1940 31

Chapter 6 35
"A Great Sailor" - December 19, 1940...35

Chapter 7 39
Warm Springs/Lend Lease and Merry Christmas - December 27, 1940......39

Chapter 8 45
A Fireside Chat, Inauguration Day, and the State of the Union - January 10, 1941..45

Chapter 9 49
Let's Start Lend-lease - March 15, 1941.......................................49

Chapter 10 53
The Atlantic Conference – August 14, 1941 53

Chapter 11 59
The Greer And a Sad Goodbye - September 9, 1941 59

Chapter 12 63
Pearl Harbor - December 7, 1941...63

Chapter 13 67
Christmas! - December 22, 1941...67

Chapter 14 75
The Girls and a Boy - January 15, 1942 75

Chapter 15 79
Executive Order 9066 - February 19, 1942 79

Chapter 16 83

Home Front, The War, and Willie - May 1, 1942...83

Chapter 17...87

The Invasion of North Africa - November 13, 1942 87

Chapter 18...89

No Words - December 31, 1942 89

Chapter 19...91

Casablanca - January 28, 1943 91

Chapter 20...97

A Movie Star - April 20, 1943 97

Chapter 21...99

Everyone got on Board! - May 20, 1943...99

Chapter 22...103

A Victory Garden - June 7, 1943 103

Chapter 23...105

Another Day Another Conference - August 25, 1943.....................................105

Chapter 24...109

Cairo, Tehran, Then Back Home - December 10, 1943 109

Chapter 25...113

General Patton, Operation Fortitude and D-day - March 15, 1943............113

Chapter 26...117

FDR's Health - February 6, 1944..117

Chapter 27...119

Election, Trip to Alaska, and the Aleutian Islands - August 31, 1944........119

Chapter 28...123

Quebec Conference and the Fala Speech - September 30, 1944 123

Chapter 29...125

Campaigning and Election Day – October 21, 1944......................................125

Chapter 30...127

Buttons - January 2, 1945..127

Chapter 31...131

The Election and Inauguration Day - January 20, 1945...............................131

Chapter 32...133

Yalta - February 5, 1945...133

Chapter 33...137

Meeting with Saudi King Abdul Aziz - February 14, 1945...........................137

Chapter 34...141

The Speech Before Congress and Continued Bad News - March 12, 1945 141

Chapter 35 145

April 12, 1945 145

Chapter 36 149

Losing my best friend, The Funeral, And A Broken Heart - April 20, 1945 149

Chapter 37 151

Leadership - June 7, 1945 151

Epilogue 155

About the Author 157

Bibliography 159

Acknowledgments

A special thanks to the Cuff Links Club for all your love and Support: Barbara August, Theresa Bischak, Maryanne Cowen, Keven Oldenburg, and William George.

Also, a special thanks to the Franklin D Roosevelt Presidential Library and Museum for all their help with my research.

To Winston, who was the voice and inspiration for Fala. I will always love you.

Introduction

My name is Fala, and I am a ten-year-old Scottish terrier who became the First Dog when I was adopted by President Franklin Roosevelt. I was considered the most loved

pet during World War II. I lived in the White House since I was six months old during the Roosevelt administration. My master, who I will proudly call Franklin, was one of the greatest presidents ever lived. I was very close the Franklin Roosevelt, and we shared an exceptional relationship. I was cute and performed tricks, and I got what I wanted from him. There was also common respect and a partnership; he was my best friend.

My years in the White House with the Roosevelts were during world history's most turbulent times. Franklin, along with his wife Eleanor, led our country with strength and courage.

Many people have written books about the Roosevelts, but my story is quite different. I was an eyewitness to history. I knew Franklin and Eleanor during the best and worst of times. I was invited to attend important meetings, went on presidential trips, and met with leaders worldwide. As I sat under a chair or begged for table scraps and pretended to be sleeping in my bed, I was listening. This is the story of World War II through my eyes.

Chapter 1

Introduction and a Hot Dog Picnic - August 8, 1940

Margaret was talking on the telephone, and I just had to listen to the news of the day. I went to my bed; it was the preferred place to be. It was warm and comfortable and my favorite place to take a nap. My ears raised when I heard that she was ordering food, dishes, glasses, and chairs. Hot Dogs, hamburgers, chicken, and steak. Oh, how my taste buds were salivating! When Margaret was finished with the orders, she excitedly phoned a friend. She said, "We are having a big party, and the President will be in attendance. I want this party to be completely casual. Just like an old-time barbecue. At this party, Big Boy will meet Mr. Roosevelt."

Trying to keep my composure, I started to pace the floor while thinking, and my mind started to wander. What type of person is he? Is he friendly? Will he give me the attention I need? My mind was beginning to race with so many questions with no answers.

An interesting thought came to my mind. What type of person becomes the President of the United States? In the dog world, the leader of the pack is usually the strongest male, and Mr. Roosevelt is the leader of the American pack.

The training had been going on for quite some time, and my confidence was high. Performing all the tricks that Margaret taught me was easy, but as First Dog, I was unsure what my role would be. How would I use my experiences to settle my apprehension about my new life to come? I was soon to find out my worry was unnecessary.

It was August 8, 1940, the sun was shining, and the weather was warm. People started to come to Wilderstein, a little at a time. I was so overwhelmed I could not even enjoy the smell of the cooked food. While wandering outside, where most of the guests were, I looked at the people's faces and tried to guess who Mr. Roosevelt was. Simultaneously, while walking through a maze of people's legs, I noticed a group of men standing and looking around. These men, who I learned were called the Secret Service, were huddled in a circle. They said that only certain guests would be allowed to see the Boss. I could only assume they were talking about the President. The Boss would be one of my favorite nicknames for Mr. Roosevelt. While walking past the men, I saw Margaret talking with a man seated in a chair. The people surrounding him laughed and joked. The man was smiling with a long cigarette holder in his mouth.

Margaret called me over.

"Big Boy, come here. This is Franklin Roosevelt, the President of the United States."

My instinct said to do what came naturally. I jumped on his lap and started to lick his face. The President petted me and laughed so hard; he began to cough. Franklin raised me, and we were nose-to-nose. with each other. I gave him a lick on the lips, and our friendship was sealed.

"Margaret, I love this little fellow. He is perfect for the job! How far into his training is he? I want to name him Fala," said the President as he was playing with me.

You must be thinking about where the name of Fala originated. An ancestor of the Roosevelt family was named Murray of Fala Hill. Fala Hill was the town's name in Scotland in which Murray lived. Murray immigrated from Scotland quite some time ago. My name was to be Murray, the Outlaw of Fala hill. Where the "Outlaw" came from is unknown. I was to be known as Fala. I like the name, but, in a way, I favored the Outlaw part; it showed my rebellious spirit!

After the picnic, we all returned to Wilderstein for more training. In a few weeks, my body grew bigger and stronger. My new diet was eggs with milk for breakfast and real meat for dinner. Dog biscuits were my reward when my behavior was perfect.

One thing I had to learn was not to bark often. That is a tough thing to do. Knowing when to bark could be confusing; I must keep my voice low so no one would be disturbed. Every day was a new learning experience.

After many months of training, Margaret thought it would be time to visit Springwood, the President's home at Hyde Park, New York. I was very excited about this visit. Springwood would eventually become my home. I know that I had to be on my best behavior on this visit, and everything had to be perfect. I was about to start my job with the President

Chapter 2

Springwood at Hyde Park - November 30, 1940

The awaited phone call came. The President's Secretary, Missy LeHand, called. The Boss would be visiting Hyde Park in late November. He wanted to use this time to get acquainted with the family and staff at Springwood. Soon afterward, I would be traveling to the White House.

It was a chilly November day; the leaves were almost off the trees. While chasing a rabbit when I heard Margaret call me.

Fala! Let's go bye-bye!

I love to go for rides in the car. My favorite words were bye-bye. My ears would automatically perk up! I ran to the car as fast as I could and jumped in. The roads were long and winding and eventually turned onto the main highway. This was the trip I was waiting for. I had to be patient because there were so many traffic lights. It took forever to get there!

Soon Margaret made a right turn into a long driveway. The gravel road made a funny noise as we drove closer to the big house. All of a sudden, a high-pitched voice which had a musical tone said,

"Hello, Margaret!"

While turning around, I saw the President's wife, Eleanor. She was a very tall woman with strong features and a friendly smile.

Eleanor said, "Where is he?"

She walked over to the car to pick me up and said,

"Margaret, he is a wonderful little one."

She put me down, and we all walked into the house. We were standing in the foyer, and all the people were having a conversation. So, I took advantage and started to look around the house. On the wall were a lot of naval ship prints and political cartoons. A collection of stuffed birds and animals was in a cabinet to the left. I looked at each one and thought to myself; they look like a bunch of live statues. They were scary, but I could not help looking at them.

Eleanor called me, "Fala, Come and meet the President!"

We all walked down the hallway and entered the library. The President was sitting in a corner at his desk, looking at his stamp collection. I ran over to him and started to wag my tail, and walked in circles.

Franklin bent over and started to pet me and said, "Welcome to Springwood, ole boy."

While Franklin proceeded to speak to Margaret about taking care of me, I thought it would be an excellent opportunity to look around the room. My curious side wanted to see everything! The library is a massive room with many books and chairs. The room was dark, which gave it a relaxed feeling. Did Franklin read all these books? I could tell the library was his favorite room. When he found time away from his presidential duties, he played with his stamp collection in the library or built a model naval ship. An older woman passed me and went right to the President.

Is that him?" she said.

"Yes," said Franklin, let me introduce you to Fala."

I ran to the older woman. She picked me up and started to pet me.

"He is a darling little one," she said with a smile on her face.

This person was Sara Roosevelt, the President's mother.

Sara called the household staff for tea to be served in the library. I sat next to Franklin, who was making silly faces at me. He was funny, and I barked back at him. Then, everyone started to laugh as he patted my head.

Several women came into the library with tea and cookies. Everyone walked over to the chairs where tea was being served. I noticed that Franklin was still sitting in his chair. Soon afterward, his chair started to magically move. His chair had wheels which he pushed with his arms.

He slowly made his way over to the table where tea was served. Mother Sara offered to help Franklin.

"You should know better, mother." Eleanor smiled and said, "helping him makes him feel helpless."

It took me a while to understand this, but the President did not have the use his legs. I was soon to find out what had happened.

Chapter 3

Polio - November 28, 1940

I was inquisitive and needed to know why Franklin could not use his legs. The great secret was all around us. Franklin had a disease called Polio. This subject of Polio was never discussed; the term disabled was never used. I found out about the great secret while sitting under the table in the sunroom at Hyde Park.

It was rather a beautiful lazy day, and I decided to sit at Eleanor's feet and listen to today's conversation. Today, a special person was joining Eleanor for tea. Her name was Clementine Churchill, wife of the Prime Minister of Great Britain. Unfortunately, as the ladies were sipping their tea, I started to drift asleep when the question I had been waiting for was asked.

"Eleanor, how did Franklin contact Polio?"

My ears perked up. I wanted to hear this story!

"Well, Franklin was a big fan of the Boy Scouts, and a convention was being held at Bear Mountain, New York. It was 1921, and I will never forget how it happened!

After Franklin returned from the convention, our family went to our home at Campo Bello, Maine, for a vacation. Franklin just had a nice healthy swim. He got out of the water because he was tired."

Wow, I thought to myself, I cannot picture Franklin any other way but in a wheelchair!

"Later that evening, he complained of a chill and pain in his legs and back."

Eleanor continued to say that she thought he might have caught a cold from the children and did not think anything of it.

"Later, Franklin had trouble moving his legs; we were not sure what was wrong. You would never think of infantile paralysis as a diagnosis. Adults were not known for getting this disease. Mostly children were affected, and the numbers during this time were frightening. We had called the doctor, who said that it was a blood clot in the spinal area. His doctor recommended a massage. Poor Franklin was in so much pain. We soon found out that massage was the worst treatment for Polio. Even the bedsheets were too much pressure for his legs."

Eleanor continued

"When the doctors finally gave the correct diagnosis, we had to keep the children away for fear of them contracting the disease.

Franklin was soon fitted for braces in Boston. He was never able to stand or move his lower body without support from the braces and a person holding his arm."

My heart sank when I heard this. I imagined Franklin lying in his bed crying in pain, helpless, with no foreseeable cure in sight. All of his strength was gone, and his children were taken away. He did not know what the future held. What a scary situation!

My anxiety about being the First Dog seems silly, considering what Franklin went through. However, I was interested in knowing how he worked through this illness.

When Eleanor came back with more cookies, the story continued.

"Franklin got a call from a New York Banker named George Peabody. He said there was a resort named Warm Springs in Georgia. The waters there had minerals and were naturally heated. There were reports that a boy afflicted with Polio could stand in the water without assistance. The news naturally aroused Franklin's curiosity, and before we knew it, we were on the train to Georgia. When we arrived at Warm Springs, the place looked terrible. It was all run down, with dirt roads and awful food. Also, the racial laws of the State of Georgia made me very upset. The people that lived in the area were so poor it was sinful."

For some reason, I could imagine Franklin living in these

conditions if he thought he could reach his goal of walking again. This experience had a significant effect on his life and his politics.

"I heard of the racial laws," said Clementine, but how did you manage in such conditions?"

Eleanor continued, "When I saw Franklin in the water, swimming and being independent, it was worth it. Louie Howe, Franklin's Assistant, was determined to get him back into politics. He said he would keep politics on the back burner and let him find his way. We had a cottage built on the grounds, which eventually led to buying Warm Springs. Soon, he was able to walk independently in the water, and through physical therapy, Franklin was able to walk with the use of braces and a person holding his arm."

At the time, disabled people were not considered capable, yet Franklin was the leader of millions of people. This was somewhat complicated for a dog to understand.

Learning how Franklin had overcome his inability to walk and win over the American people was amazing. Some people did know the President had Polio, but few knew the extent of the disability. As long as Franklin stood on the podium, smiled, and gave that Roosevelt charm, people overlooked Polio and saw the man.

I knew there was some secret or device which helped Franklin walk. As I watched Franklin, I noticed he had no use of his lower body. He needed the assistance of his braces to walk. He always had one of his sons by his side when he walked. He would walk arm and arm, locked at the elbows for extra support. He used his upper body to move his legs, which took tremendous upper body strength. Each step was an incredible effort. While his body was struggling to walk, he never once stopped smiling. I knew right then he was much stronger than most people.

There was also one unwritten rule at the White House regarding the President's public image. Photographers were not allowed to take pictures of Franklin in his wheelchair. Photos were of the President being carried or lifted by the Secret Service were prohibited. The President had to be strong and in complete control. The White House came up with very interesting ways to hide his paralysis. When Franklin made a speech, he depended on a podium for support. His speeches were filmed with Franklin behind a desk or a table. The Secret Service even drove him in a car to greet people. I could not imagine how frustrating this must have been, but the Boss would never give up. I know he would have done anything just to be able to walk again.

Franklin always had a lot of people around him. In every aspect of his life that involved physical movement, someone had to help him. If he were to bathe, get dressed, go to the bathroom, get in and out of a car, his staff would be available to assist him. Likewise, the President's Assistants had to plan every public appearance carefully.

I never thought that Franklin had any fears until the Boss thought he smelled smoke one night. He called for some assistance, but no one was nearby. Franklin had a panicked look on his face. He rolled off the bed and dragged himself out into the hallway. I ran as fast as I could to get some help. The valet on duty brought Franklin back to his room and assured him that everything was ok. The Boss admitted that fire was the biggest fear of his life. He ordered the bedroom door to be opened at all times, and a valet or the Secret Service were to be stationed outside of his bedroom. The idea of fire consuming him and his inability to escape was too overwhelming for him. From this moment on, I took the job of making sure that all was well at night. I stayed awake many nights, ensuring everything was in order while the President slept. We were best friends; this was the least I could have done. In one way, I did feel sorry for him, but his disability made him a strong, compassionate person. That is why he became President.

Chapter 4

Hyde Park, and New York City, New York - December 3, 1940

I was walking around the house trying to find the kitchen when Franklin called me as he was wheeling himself towards me.

"Would you like to go for a ride?"

I was trying to understand what he meant. While walking next to the wheelchair into the foyer, I heard him say,

"Come, Fala, let's go upstairs."

There was no way for Franklin to get up those stairs.

Maybe his chair has some sort of magic! My mind started to race, coming up with all kinds of possibilities. Finally, I stopped at the stairs and turned around.

"Oh no, Fala, he said, come here."

I decided I should let Franklin lead the way. So we went to the staircase, and he stopped his wheelchair.

"Jump on my lap, ole boy."

I hesitated because I thought I would hurt him. I jumped and started to lick his face. The President then backed his chair into a closet. This was very strange, but I knew the Boss was up to something. Franklin then lifted his arms and started to pull on a rope. The closet started to jerk and then moved upward.

"Don't worry, Fala, it is my way of climbing the stairs and keeping in shape."

My heart was pounding so hard that I thought it would explode. We reached the second floor, the closet jerked, the door opened, and Franklin wheeled us out. We rolled down the corridor. We stopped by the window and saw the winding hills and beautiful trees. One of the President's valets came to greet us and asked,

"Would the boss like an afternoon nap?"

"Why yes, I do indeed!" said Franklin.

When the Boss was put in the bed, I heard,

"Fala, come here."

I sat at the edge of the bed, wagging my tail, ready to listen to the following command.

"Come on the bed, ole boy, but don't tell anyone."

I jumped onto the bed and rested my head on Franklin's chest, and we both fell asleep.

We awakened after an hour. When the valet came to attend to Franklin, I thought this was an excellent opportunity to get acquainted with the house. The first place I wanted to see was the kitchen. The sounds of dishes being washed, and the smell of good food cooking gave me every indication that the kitchen was downstairs right down the hall. As I walked into the kitchen, one of the staff said,

"This is Fala, the President's new dog. Isn't he a cute one?"

Afterward, they all started to pet me and said, welcome to the family.

Dinner was about to be served, and all were waiting for Franklin to come downstairs. It took him a long time, so I ran up the stairs and saw everybody coming down the corridor. I jumped onto the wheelchair, went downstairs in our favorite closet, and proceeded to the dining room. I jumped down and went under the table, waiting for scraps and to listen to all the jokes and stories of the day.

After dinner was over, Franklin said to one of the staff, "Fala needs to eat! So, I bought him a new dog dish and water bowl."

I will never forget the first time I saw my new bowl. It shined like a new penny. It was a deep red with the letters D_O_G written across the bowl. The dish was filled with dog food. I would rather have eaten some leftovers from dinner, but dog food will do. After I was finished my dinner, I was immediately taken out by the Secret Service for a walk.

Even though I was housebroken, I was still young and prone to accidents.

The outdoors was scary at first but exploring was something I wanted to do. Even though I was tempted, I was scared to take the chance again. My new leash, which was made of leather and was quite strong. I could not wait until the time came when I would be able to run off on my own.

Franklin was waiting on the porch when I was running around outside. Deep in the back of his mind, I know he would have loved to have walked me.

In the evening, everyone gathered in the library for coffee and dessert. The Boss was in his favorite part of the room, sitting by his desk and looking at his stamp collection. He could sit for hours looking at stamps from all over the world.

When the coffee was being served, Eleanor said,

"Franklin, why don't you join us."

The Boss replied, "I think I will take my coffee here and relax."

Eleanor then said, "Fala, would you then join us?"

I was starting to feel right at home.

As First Dog, it was my duty to wake Franklin up with a lick to the face.

"Fala, you know how to make me happy. I have great plans for you, ole boy. You are going to become the most famous dog in the world!"

My day started with a nice walk by a couple of Secret Service agents. They loved to play with me. We would play catch and let me run without my leash. When I returned to the house, I ate my breakfast and returned outside for another walk. Wow! I had never had so many people pay attention to me.

In the afternoon, Franklin decided he wanted to take a drive in his car. I wondered how he could drive without the use of his legs. The President's car was fitted with a unique device to operate the vehicle using his hands. I met two other staff members who were ready to go for a ride. Missy Leland and Grace Tully were the President's Secretaries who were always ready for a trip in the car. We also were followed by the Secret Service and the police.

As we were driving, Franklin said, "Let's have some fun."

He speeded up the car and did a fast U-Turn. All the vehicles following us could not keep up and got lost. I was scared out of my skin! But we were all laughing in the car, having a good time. I soon realized the Boss liked mischief just as much as I did.

The next day Margaret came to Springwood to bring me back to Wilderstein for more training. I ran to her and wagged my tail as hard as possible upon entering the house. The President suggested that I was a great addition, and he would want me as part of his Cabinet!

The next training was in the big city. I was used to a wide-open environment with a lot of room to run. The President wanted me to be able to handle crowds and the photographers. So back to Wildenstein for a few days. I

spent most of the day chasing squirrels, laying in the sun and training, and then onto the big city.

Margaret took me to the car and drove on the highway for a long time. The further we went, we saw fewer trees and more buildings. There were people everywhere, cars stopping and going, horns beeping, and police sirens. Just looking out the window, everything seemed so different and confusing. It looked like we were in another country. I knew I had a lot to learn in a short amount of time.

When we got to Margaret's house in the city, she put me on a leash.

"Fala, things are different here. You cannot run by yourself here. There is a nice park across the way. I will make sure you go for a walk there every day. We are staying for three weeks, and in that time, you will learn to be a city dog. The city will take some getting used to. People will always be around. There are many cars, bicycles, busses, and taxis. You must be aware of your surroundings at all times."

As I got out of the car could not believe how tall the buildings were. They looked like they were growing out of each other. There were trees here but nothing like the country. The city is mysterious yet wonderful at the same time. One thing I did notice, people were always going someplace. Some were walking fast, but some were walking slow. All the cars were going in the same direction, driving fast to get to some destination.

During this time, I learned to ride in a car with a lot of traffic. Stop-and-go traffic was the worst. My stomach would turn all the time, but the more I was in the car, the better it started to feel.

My first train ride was at Penn Station in Midtown Manhattan. I had to ride in the baggage car in a crate. I was not happy about this. Margaret assured me this was for training purposes only. I had to get used to the motion of the train. Margaret told me when traveling with the President, my seat would be right next to Franklin. I would be by his side.

Our stay in New York went by very fast. We got on the train again, but it was to be a long trip this time. I was in the baggage car, and I could not see where we were going.

Finally, the train stopped, and the baggage handler gave me to Margaret. As I walked off the train, I saw Franklin in his blue car waiting for us. I was home at Hyde Park!

My time in Springwood was full of learning my routines and duties. Every morning the President was given his breakfast with a dog biscuit on his tray. I was to perform several tricks to earn my tasty treat. I learned to roll over, sit up and shake hands. My job was to make the President happy. It was a win, win situation for both of us. I made Franklin laugh, and I got to eat a cookie.

While exploring the house, I learned where my treats were kept and which kitchen staff would give me leftovers. That was a lot of fun.

I often wondered how Franklin was able to contact his valet if he needed help. One day I saw a small light on the wall. I went over to investigate, and there was a black box with several lights. Every light represented a room in the house. If a light came on, it would give the Boss's location. The Secret Service would go to the room and assist him. Just leave it up to Franklin to have everything figured out!

Soon Margaret and I returned to Wilderstein for more training. I was not too happy about going back. I was getting far more attention at Springwood. Wilderstein did not have the excitement of Springwood but did have some good qualities. The land was right along the Hudson River. I would watch the water flow down the river many afternoons and dream about my future.

Margaret told me on the morning of November 2 that I was going to Springwood and that I should be on my best behavior. It was election night in Hyde Park. This election would determine if Franklin would remain President of the United States. Margaret told me that everyone would be nervous, and it was my job to loosen everyone up.

It was a cool evening outside, but the house was warm inside. It was crowded in the house, and the situation was tense. The sounds of ticker tape machines were deafening. Upon my arrival, Eleanor told us that Franklin wanted to be alone. The election results were pouring in, and this would be my opportunity to ease the tension.

Everyone talked, and their expressions looked positive, so I assumed everything was going well. While strolling into the dining room, the Boss was sitting in a chair looking at tally sheets. He said,

"Fala ole boy! Glad to see you are here."

Eleanor walked into the room. "Franklin, you are sweating so much. Should I call the doctor?"

"No, I'm just nervous; I wish I had the final results!" said Franklin.

I started to roll on the floor and performed tricks.

"Now that is just what I needed, Fala! Thank you so much!" said the President.

At this point, no one knew how the election would turn out. As the night went on, we all looked out the window and saw shining lights coming towards the house from Albany Post Road.

Eleanor said, "My God, look at our supporters!"

The people who voted for the President who lived in Hyde Park came with railroad flairs and signs. They shouted Roosevelt for President! Franklin permitted the supporters to enter the estate. The closer the light came to the house, the more beautiful they looked. Five hundred people were shouting and clapping, wanting to see the President.

Eleanor thought it would be an excellent idea for the family to address the crowd. I thought I would have a first-rate seat looking from the window. But, to my surprise, Franklin called me.

"Fala, let's go outside and say hello to America!"

Franklin walked with his son James on one arm and a cane. Eleanor put me on a leash, and we call proceeded outside. It was so cold, and my legs were shaking. I wagged my tail as the newly elected President addressed the crowd. Afterward, we all came inside, and I heard,

"Fala ole boy, soon you are going to be a star!"

Chapter 5

Washington, D.C. and The White House - November 17, 1940

November was coming soon, and I was getting ready for the big trip. The dog dishes had to be packed, and my coat and leashes were put in my special bag. Before I knew it, I was on the train headed for Washington, D.C.

Once again had to ride in the baggage car. Being in a crate was rather annoying. It was cold and damp, and the swaying of the train was starting to make me sick. The thought that I would be traveling with Franklin instead, I was in a crate.

We finally arrived at Union Station in Washington, D.C. A special car was waiting to take us to the White House. The city of Washington has many large buildings. It strangely reminded me of New York, yet the city was very different.

Many buildings were white like snow; some were so pretty that they looked like birthday cakes. Finally, the car started to slow down, and there was The White House! We drove up the long driveway and pulled over to the side of the building. I remember being overwhelmed by its grandeur.

Margaret brought me to the Oval Office. On the way, I was slipping on the bare floor, and I made sure to walk on the rugs. We had to wait outside the Oval Office until Franklin was ready to see us.

A Presidential Aide told us it was time to enter. Margaret removed my leash as I walked in, and I ran under the desk as fast as possible. I heard his voice.

"Fala ole boy" Welcome to the White House!"

It was the Boss! As soon as he started to pet me, I began to jump and do tricks. Margaret walked me over to the kitchen and introduced the White House staff. The kitchen was big, and so many people walked in and out. I noticed that my dog dish was sitting on the counter. Everyone was glad to meet me. The Head Butler, Alonzo Fields, was the first person I met.

"Hello, Mr. Fala; it is my pleasure to meet you on this nice fine day."

Mr. Fields was always polite, yet he could run the White House staff like the military. Everything was always on time and in its place. I still found it remarkable that Mr. Fields could put together the grandest party in a matter of a few hours. The guests always had plenty of food under Mr.

Field's watch. The White House cook, Mrs. Nesbit, was in charge of the meals served. When she was cooking the food at the White House, it was a national scandal. More on that later.

The President had so many staff members it was hard to remember their names. The people I encountered were all in the inner circle of the White House. Of course, I also must include the household staff, and of course, the chief and servants were always my favorite.

Missy LeHand, the President's private secretary, was a familiar face at Hyde Park. Missy was a very valuable employee who devoted her life to the President. She had worked for the Roosevelts before Franklin contracted polio. Missy thought of herself as the President's second wife.

Everyone knew when Miss LeHand gave an order, the White House staff would make sure that her wishes were granted. We all knew that Franklin would always back her up. Missy took an interest in what Eleanor did not have the time for.

She was responsible for arranging the President's most prized possession, his stamp collection. When Franklin would get a new stamp, the first person he shared his new find was Missy. She shared his enthusiasm for his hobbies and was a great companion. Missy also knew how to make the President laugh, and she made us all have a great time. One thing I could say about Missy; she had a lot of guts. Missy used to love to take car rides with Franklin. I have to be honest; FDR was a great

President, but he was a lousy driver. No one wanted to go in the car with him; none of his children, Eleanor, or mother would dare to go near the Ford. Not Missy! I think she looked forward to her rides with Franklin. I went on a few of these adventures. While I was getting sick in the front seat, Franklin and Missy would be laughing, having a grand time.

The one relationship that never ceased to amaze me was the President and the White House cook Mrs. Henrietta Nesbitt. Eleanor met Mrs. Nesbitt in Hyde Park while shopping for a loaf of whole wheat bread. She started talking to Mrs. Nesbitt and found that they had a lot in common.

Henrietta was a Woman's Voter organization member, and soon afterward, the two ladies became friends. Mrs. Nesbitt was a widow who owned the bakery where the infamous bread was bought. Eleanor, who was so kind-hearted, requested that Mrs. Nesbitt join her at the White House and soon became the White House cook.

Franklin hated Mrs. Nesbitt's cooking. The food was plain and simple. The President enjoyed dishes that were exotic at that time. Quail and duck were his favorites, yet he was always willing to try something new. Mrs. Nesbitt's cooking was repetitive, very plain, with no taste. The meals were usually overcooked. Numerous complaints were made about the food. The President would write memos to his staff and Mrs. Nesbitt about what he liked to eat and which foods he did not. If one person would make Franklin's blood boil, it was Mrs. Nesbitt. I remember one week, chicken was on the menu every day. Every time the staff brought out chicken, I could see the Boss's face slowly turn red. While the rift between Franklin and Mrs. Nesbitt was quite funny, there was a side to this relationship that bothered me. Due to his polio, the President was dependent on his staff for all of his needs. There was no way the President could go out to eat. He could not dine at a restaurant because he did not want the public to see him in a wheelchair. At one point, Mrs.

Nesbitt's cooking caused him to lose weight. One day Franklin was so frustrated after eating sweetbreads seven days in a row he wrote a memo to her stating that he did not want sweetbreads served for several months. He also did not like broccoli and wrote a memo stating he did not wish to have this vegetable served. The next day broccoli was on his plate. She said it was good for him and he should eat it.

Many White House staff members would not eat Mrs. Nesbitt's cooking, either. Instead, many staff members could be seen making scrambled eggs for dinner in the kitchen.

Franklin, one day, was waiting to be served his dinner. I walked into the dining room, and Franklin said to me, "I wonder what brew Mrs. Nesbitt is preparing? Fala, I envy you; I bet the dog food tastes better.'

The chicken was served with broccoli with rolls and no butter a few minutes later. Franklin started to cut the meat and threw down his fork and knife.

"Eleanor! Can't this woman make anything I can eat?" Even Fala is not interested in my dinner."

Franklin then instructed a staff member to go out somewhere and get something good to eat. He then sent a letter to Mrs. Nesbitt that a fowl should be plucked before cooking so the meat is not dry. The Boss always used to say that if a fowl was given to me, Mrs. Nesbitt would find a way to ruin it. The President's son Elliot called the food at the White House a national scandal. He would say her cooking was tasteless without variety. Very soon, the word spread about the White House cuisine. Many guests would have eaten before being invited for dinner. I was lucky; I had dog food for dinner!

Many people wanted to see the President; I hardly spent any time with him that night. One day while I was napping in the back of the Oval Office, as an important meeting was taking place, I drifted off to sleep and made a loud whimper. Everyone started to laugh, and Franklin said,

"Fala ole boy, I feel like I need a vacation. Would you like to come with me?"

I started to wag my tail with excitement! Little did I know this would be my first appearance as the First Dog.

Chapter 6

"A Great Sailor" - December 19, 1940

On December 2, 1940, I would be making my first appearance as the First Dog. Franklin told me that we were going to the West Indies on an inspection cruise. I was so excited! I thought this was an excellent opportunity to spend time with Franklin.

We departed from Washington, D.C., on December 2 and took a train to Miami, Florida. When we got to Union Station, there were photographers and reporters. They were all interested to know where we were going. As we boarded the train, I learned that the President had a special carriage called the Ferdinand Magellan. I was placed on a seat right next to Franklin. No more crates and baggage trains for me. I sat right next to the President, and I cuddled up against his side as he petted me. I was presented with a new dog collar and a tag that said "Fala; The White House." I was so proud to be the President's best friend and to be representing our great country.

The trip's official purpose was to see first-hand the naval bases constructed in British territory. As time went on, I sensed that Franklin had other ideas. I knew how much he loved the sea. The Boss saw this trip as a mini vacation. The President's doctor thought the trip would give him the rest that he needed and lift his spirits. This trip was not given a lot of publicity. The only one invited on the White House journey was Harry Hopkins, the President's Chief Advisor.

We were on the train on the way to Florida. We slept in the sleeper car together. I made sure I found a good spot to sleep. I slept on Franklin's feet to keep them warm.

After we arrived in Miami, Florida, we boarded a cruiser named the Tuscaloosa, pulled from active duty just for the President. Two destroyers called the May-Rant, and the Tripp went along for the ride.

Before we boarded the ship, The President held a press conference from his car. So, I would be meeting with the press for the first time.

Franklin acknowledged the crowd with all of his charm. We then proceeded to board the ship and were greeted with full honors. As we made our way to the ship's deck, the Presidential Flag was hoisted, and a 21-gun salute was given. That is one tradition that I had such a hard time with. Dogs have very sensitive ears, and the sound gave me such a headache. When I looked up at Franklin, I could see that the sound bothered his ears also. There were huge crowds of people waving as the ship was taking off. I never saw so many cameras in my life. Franklin was standing on the edge of the boat near a huge wall. I managed to wiggle my way to a hole to see all those wonderful people. Young girls with bobby socks and boys with slicked-back hair were jumping up and down to get a glimpse of the President. The sailors dropped the ropes, lifted the anchors, and before I knew it, we were on our way to Guantanamo Bay, Cuba! We spent the rest of the afternoon shaking hands and greeting the crew.

When we arrived in Cuba, the President had several meetings. At their conclusion, the President asked one of the Naval Aides to go ashore to get him some Cuban cigars.

Franklin said they were the best in the world.

"Buy enough for me and all of my staff as well as the personnel of the Tuscaloosa."

That is one thing I loved about Franklin; he always thought of others when he was thinking about himself.

While we were in Jamaica, Franklin requested a whaleboat to go fishing. The President of The United States was sitting in a wicker chair with a white hat. I laughed at the sun visor, which was built into the hat. We all had a great time.

Even though the fish weren't biting that day, there was always something to discuss. The few fish that were caught were lying on the boat's deck, jumping up and down. I could see that everyone was a little quiet at one point, so I started to dance just like the fish. Everyone laughed as Harry said,

"There is never a dull moment with this little pup around!"

During his stops at various islands in the Caribbean, Franklin met with multiple dignitaries to discuss political matters. I found myself bored while these meetings were going on. So, I decided to go upstairs to the top deck to feel the breeze in my face. I saw a row of sailors sleeping, taking in the sun on such a beautiful day. My ear popped up, and I thought it would be fun to lick their toes as I walked down the row. None of the sailors had shoes on, so I started my mischief, and soon after, all the sailors were laughing.

On December 7, 1940' we were docked at the Aves Island, and I noticed an airplane landing on the water. This plane had balloons instead of wheels. The aircraft landed on the water and did not sink! I was told this was the mail plane, and a small boat was sent to the plane to pick up the mail.

"Look at that, Fala! The mail is here! Maybe there will be a letter from Eleanor!

There were letters from many different people, but there was one letter Franklin could not stop reading. He was sitting on the deck, opening his mail, and saw a letter from "Ole Winnie." Winston Churchill, The Prime Minister of Great Britain. As he started to read this letter, Franklin's face changed. His tone was serious and stern. I had never seen anything like this before. I began to take an interest in the world's situation as I saw Franklin's disturbed face.

Adolph Hitler, the leader of Nazi Germany, had invaded several countries in Europe. Currently, Germany was invading France with Great Britain on its mind. Next, Churchill wrote the President a letter about the British situation. He said that while Britain could handle the air attacks, they were running out of materials needed to fight the war. Churchill further stated that the British people were ready to suffer economically;

they could not keep fighting without help from the United States. England required cash and needed help very soon. They would no longer be able to pay for shipping and supplies. They only had two billion dollars to pay for five billion dollars worth of American factories' orders. The letter had a significant effect on Franklin. He would sit on the deck and just stare out to the sea. I was sitting next to him; I would feel his hand stroke the top of my head. I knew he was in deep thought.

The war in Europe was always on the President's mind. People in the United States thought it best to keep out of this war. Franklin was able to see beyond this. He knew if Great Britain were to fall, Nazi occupation was only a step closer. We had only the Atlantic Ocean separating us. Throughout the rest of the trip in true Roosevelt fashion, he asked the crew if he could stay on the deck and be alone with his thoughts. I was the only one allowed to be with him. I knew the times were changing fast, very fast.

Our trip went by quickly, even though the fish weren't biting. Franklin even received a radiogram from the famous writer Ernest Hemingway who said good fishing was in the Mona Passage between Puerto Rico and the Dominican Republic. Franklin would always joke that the fish knew we were coming!

On Saturday, December 14, 1940, our trip ended when we docked in Charleston, South Carolina. The President gave a news conference from our private cabin onboard the ship.

All reporters were trying to get the best scoop. As Franklin addressed the press, he would lean over and stroke my head. One reporter asked, "How did Fala do on the trip?"

Franklin answered, "he is a great sailor, one fine sailor!"

Chapter 7

Warm Springs/Lend Lease and Merry Christmas - December 27, 1940

As we left the Tuscaloosa, the ship gave us another 21- gun salute. We parted and were on our way to Warm Springs, Georgia. Franklin looked so rested, but he had a look of concern on his face. I have heard so much about Warm Springs from all the people at Hyde Park. Some liked it, and some did not. Eleanor disliked going to Warm Springs not because it was such a terrible place but because of Georgia's racial laws. It bothered her to see water fountains and bathrooms marked "white or colored only." These were the product of the racist attitudes of the time. Sara disliked Warm Springs because it confirmed her son's disability.

Warm Springs was like a vacation spot. It was relaxing, serene, and just beautiful. My first visit was only one day, but it was lots of fun. I wanted to play with the children, but their disabilities prevented them. I had to adapt a way I would able to play with them. Many of them were just like Franklin, unable to use their limbs. Yet, they were brave and confronted their illnesses with strength and dignity. People who came to Warm Springs did not come for vacation. They came because of the water. The water had a high concentration of minerals and a warm temperature, enabling people with polio to exercise and use their muscles. They also could stay in the water for long periods without getting cold.

Franklin loved Warm Springs. He always said it was one of his favorite places in the world. When Franklin came down to Georgia, a world existed that he had not seen before in the early years. Franklin saw poverty, poor education, and segregation in this rural part of America. The Boss learned to communicate with the average person during the early years. It was a learning process, and soon he understood their needs and concerns. Many programs from the New Deal had their origins from the experiences at Warm Springs.

As we drove up the entrance, I got my first view of the "Little White House." It looked like a vacation cabin with a wood interior and simple and plain furniture. It had one floor surrounded by trees. I knew Franklin still had his fears of fire. One level home relieved his anxiety.

Franklin wanted to have a Thanksgiving dinner with the patients staying there. The President of the United States was sitting with children with polio, having a good time laughing and making jokes. The Boss carved the turkey like a pro and ensured everyone got a piece. I sat under the table and enjoyed the turkey from the hands that came from under the table. Soon afterward, we left for Washington, D.C.

We arrived at the White House on 12/16/40. After leaving the train station, my legs were wobbly; I could hardly walk. I was able to relate to the Boss's disability for the first time. But there was Franklin, ever joyful, smiling, waving to the crowd. Franklin's head was cocked back with his cigarette holder lifted towards the sky. I know he enjoyed being President.

When things got settled, Franklin introduced me to Henry Morgenthau, Secretary of the Treasury. He was the guy who was in charge of all the money. Mr. Morgenthau was a close advisor to the President.

"Henry, I would like you to meet the latest addition to the Roosevelt Family. Fala, my new puppy."

I walked around Mr. Morgenthau's legs and circled his entire body as I wagged my tail.

"Henry, I have something to discuss with you. I received a letter from the Prime Minister of Great Britain. In his letter, Mr. Churchill says that Great Britain would be on the verge of bankruptcy without the United States' help. My fear is if Great Britain falls under Nazi control, there is only an ocean between us. I feel deep in my heart that in due time Hitler will be looking to attack the United States."

Mr. Morgenthau looked very concerned. "I have to try to sell the idea to the American people," said the President.

We were about to have a meeting when Harry Hopkins entered the room. He was the President's confidant and a nice man. He had a crooked smile and always was a lot of fun. I gave Harry a bark and continued to play with my ball underneath the President's desk. The words I was about to hear changed us all.

Franklin started the meeting. I would be listening to words of such great importance for the first time. I stayed quiet and put my head on the carpet.

Harry seemed to be aware of the letter from the Prime Minister of Great Britain. The President proceeded, "I have come up with the idea that the American people will not only understand but will support. If we could lend or lease battleships, guns, and armaments to Great Britain, they could defend themselves. We could increase production and put people to work while building up our defense to meet any confrontation. We would be getting ready and helping Great Britain without getting involved in the war."

"Sounds good to me," said Harry.

But what will happen at the end of the war?"

"Well, my friend, said the President, Great Britain will just have to give everything back. If a ship is destroyed, they will have to pay for it. So, I think if we can eliminate the dollar sign, we would have a great chance of getting this passed."

"What do you want to call this?" asked Henry.

With a big smile and a cigarette holder higher than I had ever seen it, Franklin said, "Let's call this Lend-Lease."

On December 17, 1940, the President of the United States gave a press conference. He spoke of the importance of the United States and Great Britain defending themselves. He explained how to build up our production facilities and continue the munitions' flow to Great Britain.

"I am trying to eliminate the dollar sign, now that is something brand new in the thoughts of practically everybody here in this room. So, get rid of the silly foolish dollar sign."

To make the everyday man understand what this meant, he compared England's situation to something that would occur in everyday life.

The President said, "If my neighbor's house were to catch fire and I have a garden hose that he could connect with a fire hydrant, I could help my neighbor put out the fire. If I lend him the garden hose, he will give it back once the fire is out. But if the hose is damaged during the fire, my neighbor would replace it."

I thought this was brilliant! Then, finally, everyone could understand what was to happen. It was so simple that even I would vote to pass this bill.

The Roosevelts all decided to surprise the staff at Hyde Park, giving Franklin a break to be with family. We took the train to New York, which would be a ride I would become very familiar. Unfortunately, we could not spend much time in New York because we had to be in Washington on December 24 for the National Christmas Tree lighting. We arrived in Hyde Park in the afternoon, and all the relatives were there to greet us. Christmas was Eleanor's most favorite time of year. There is not one person I could think of that did not get a present. She whipped around the house to make sure everything was in order. We had a Christmas meal about midday; afterward, the fun would begin.

Franklin was sure to be directing the tree's trimming and reading the story "A Christmas Carol by Charles Dickens. The Christmas tree was so beautifully decorated with real candles. It surprised me that my friend, the man who had such a fear of fire, would use candles on his Christmas tree. That was the type of man he was; advanced in politics, old fashion in tradition. Everyone received presents, but all the children received the best gift: Scottie dog dolls. I was so surprised when I saw them. They looked so real to me. I walked up to the doll and started barking. When the doll did not bark back, I figured that this dog was not real and walked away. There is nothing like the real thing, I guess!

Eleanor distributed all the presents to the staff, and before I knew it, we were back on the train on our way to Washington.

Christmas at the White House was always special. The President invited the whole Roosevelt family, Harry Hopkins and his five-year-old daughter Diana to partake in the festivities. Diana took it upon herself to be my friend during all the ceremonies. She held my leash and played with me while Eleanor and Franklin tended to their guests. We all went to the East Room for the first part of the ceremony. The tree selected was trimmed with white and silver and sparked many colors as the lights twinkled. Everyone had a Christmas stocking stuffed with goodies as we walked into the room. My stocking was hung in the center with big letters spelled; FALA. Diana was sure to show everyone both of our stockings. Mr. Fields told us that the tree outside the White House would soon be lit. The President would say a few words, and then we returned to the East Room for refreshments and distributed gifts to the staff. Eleanor ran all over the White House, looking for several boxes that had forgotten to make their way under the Christmas tree. A closet upstairs was full of Christmas gifts that were supposed to be a secret. Eleanor would purchase gifts from around the world during the year and keep them hidden until Christmas Day. For some reason, every year, she forgets to put some of the presents under the tree. The secret closet was not the best-kept secret in the White House.

We all stepped onto the balcony before a crowd of 8000 well-wishers. The tree in front of the

White House was a 32-foot Cedar tree from Mount Vernon, Virginia. The tree had 700 lights and 150 twinkling stars. People from the Electric Institute and the D. C. public school decorated the tree. As we came onto the balcony, the U.S. Marine band played Christmas carols, and The Boy Scouts sang greetings to The President. Franklin pressed the switch; the Christmas tree was lit, and everyone clapped for joy. As Franklin began his speech, he had a sad look on his face. The Boss knew what faced us in the upcoming year. He told the guests before him and the millions on the radio.

"Let us make this Christmas a merry one for the little children in our midst. But, for us of mature years, it cannot be merry."

The President and his staff returned inside the White House, and refreshments were served. We also exchanged gifts. Children received toys, but the most exciting was a silver key chain of a Scottie dog. Many came up personally to me to thank me for my generosity. Everyone sat around and drank eggnog and relaxed.

The following day the family assembled in the President's bedroom to open their gifts.

Franklin said, "Fala, we usually start with the youngest, so this is your stocking."

I received a new collar with a Scottish plaid design with a bow, and a new ball. The Boss distributed all the presents, and everyone had so much fun.

Chapter 8

A Fireside Chat, Inauguration Day, and the State of the Union - January 10, 1941

It was late December, and the President wanted to bring Lend-Lease's concept to the American People. He needed to get the approval of Congress, and the best way to do this was to get the citizens involved in the process. In a Fireside Chat, the President spoke to the people as a friend. He used the garden hose as an example to have the people concretely understand the proposal. It made sense, and the people liked it.

The President felt it was in the best interest of the people to have a fireside chat to keep everyone informed about the current situation in Europe. When the time came, Franklin was in a room with several cameras pointed towards him. He did not look nervous, but I can imagine he must have been a bundle of nerves inside. The staff asked me to leave the room; all must have absolute silence.

Several cabinet members sat listening to the speech in the room next door. The broadcast came through a large brown radio which crackled at times. Everyone was tense while the President was speaking. Franklin's voice was stern and direct as he spoke about the last-ditch effort to preserve our American Independence. The President addressed the situation concerning the threat by Nazi Germany and Italy to dominate and enslave Europe. No one could even think to enter peace talks unless the Nazis abandoned all thoughts of the world's domination. He also spoke about the Empire of Japan and their conquest of China.

I thought to myself, *This is a dire situation. It would take the cooperation of all of our allies together to destroy the enemy.* But, as the speech continued, not a word was whispered by anyone in the room.

The President called for the American people to show their patriotism and courage as if we were at war. He called for increased production of all armaments. The President said, "If we sell our ships and planes to our Allies, we also will be creating a stockpile of supplies should we need them. We have no desire to get involved in this war, but we cannot be blind by going to bed and pulling the sheets above our heads. We shall be the Arsenal of Democracy."

When the chat was over, everyone congratulated him. His speech was perfect. I cannot help but think about what was on the American people's minds at this point.

It was time for the Inauguration on a cold January day.

The wind was crisp against my nose. The ground was freezing, and I felt like I was walking on ice. All the leaves were gone, and everything looked dead except the White House. The Nation was about to inaugurate President Franklin Delano Roosevelt for the third time.

I went to the President's dressing room and saw the Boss in a suit with tails. As he stood up, he reminded me of a penguin. He had a hat similar to Abraham Lincoln's. His assistants were brushing off any lint that made its way to his suit. He also had another person styling his hair. Franklin was laughing and did not show the slightest bit of nervousness.

The valet said," You should be a pro at this, Mr. President."

I ran over to Eleanor's room. She looked beautiful in her new dress. She was smiling and was very busy making sure everything was in its proper place.

Everyone was getting ready to leave. I was so proud of The President and to be witnessing such an event. Being elected three times was a charm. It was overwhelming,

The cars pulled up the long driveway. The first car stopped; I jumped in, ready to go to the Capital. The President got in the car and started to laugh,

"Fala, what are you doing in the car? Sorry old man but not this time."

Mike Reilly of the Secret Service picked me up, and the cars started to leave. I ran to the porch of the White House and began to bark.

I had never been so angry in my life! Here I was, First Dog not being invited to the Inauguration! There must have been some kind of mistake.

I wanted to go to the Capitol Building, so I took it upon myself to walk there to see what was going on. But unfortunately, no one remembered to put me in my crate, so I took it upon myself to leave the White House and stroll down the streets of Washington, D.C., to get a glimpse of the festivities.

The streets were busy with people walking and driving cars. I started to follow some people thinking they were on their way to the Capital. The crowd was going to a movie theater. It was getting colder. I was looking around, and nothing was familiar. I walked down an alleyway and sat down, trying to figure out my next move.

A nice young man came over to me and said, "Hey, little guy, are you lost?"

I started to whimper and cry. Finally, the man picked me up and looked at my dog tag.

"My God! You are Fala! The President's Dog! I think you need to be taken home."

At the White House, the staff was going crazy looking for me. They were worried and concerned about what the President would say.

The doorbell rang, and the nice young man gave me to Mr. Fields.

"Fala, you had us so worried about you! I will talk to the President and tell him how upset you were," said Mr. Fields

I was not only upset; My Scottish blood was boiling! I felt left out and rejected. I was unsure what I would do, so I headed to the kitchen to see what was going. Everyone was running around, up and down the stairs trying to get ready for the President's arrival. Mrs. Nesbit told the staff to put me in my crate.

"We cannot watch the dog and get things ready at the same time," yelled Mrs. Nesbitt.

Every time she walked by, I growled at her. I started to get tired, and I waited until the President came home.

A few hours later, I heard the Boss's voice. Everyone was laughing and talking at the same time. Franklin looked prouder than ever. He had a smile from ear to ear. Then, he turned around and saw me in the crate.

"What is this all about?"

A staff member told Franklin the story and that Mrs.

Nesbit sentenced me to prison because she was busy.

"OH NO! We cannot have this!"

I was let out of the crate and jumped on Franklin's lap. I gave him tons of kisses. When I saw Mrs. Nesbit walk by, I growled. A loud laugh came from the President, and he whispered to me, "At least you do not have to eat her cooking."

A few weeks later, the President's following speech was the State of the Union. The President talked about the Four Freedoms during this speech, which outlined the need to defend freedom worldwide. The First of the Four Freedoms was the Freedom of Speech and Expression. People were able to speak their thoughts without fear of reprisal. The Second was the Freedom to Worship God in their own way. The United States is a country where many religions are observed. Anyone who could walk into a Church, Synagogue, Mosque, or Temple can follow their faith without fear to do so. Thirdly, was the Freedom of Want.

Every American should have the right to have basic life needs. The right to an education, enough to eat, and a place to live. The Fourth was the Freedom from Fear. People should be free to say and do things without fearing the government. Also included any government that threatened the United States. These Four Freedoms became so popular that American Artist Norman Rockwell painted each freedom on canvas. Each painting was equally as powerful as were the words. When America had entered the war, each painting was featured on the Saturday Evening Post to boost morale. This speech would be one of Franklin's finest.

Chapter 9

Let's Start Lend-lease - March 15, 1941

The war in Europe had been spreading rapidly. German troops had spread throughout most of Europe, the Balkans, Greece, and Northern Africa. The United Kingdom was experiencing heavy bombing from German aircraft. England was in desperate times. They were short of food, clothing, and essential military supplies.

The letter sent by Winston Churchill never left the President's mind. He knew that if England were to fall into Nazi hands, it would be a matter of time before they would become a threat to the United States. So, after giving his fireside chat called the Arsenal of Democracy, he started to put Lend-Lease into full gear.

The first part was to sell Lend-Lease to Congress and the American people. Many people opposed the idea of helping Great Britain. They saw it as the first step into getting involved in a war. The isolationists felt we should care for America first, and the Lend-Lease bill would give too much power to Roosevelt, who could declare war worldwide.

The first thing the President had done was to send Harry Hopkins to Great Britain. The purpose of his journey was to speak with Winston Churchill, the Prime Minister, and survey the situation.

The report from Great Britain was grim. Hopkins suggested that we get Lend-Lease passed as soon as possible. The Germans destroyed large parts of London. It was time to get the isolationists interested in Lend-Lease.

In a brilliant move, the Boss sent his old rival from the last election, Wendell Willkie, to Great Britain to speak with Winston Churchill. As a

Republican, Mr. Willkie would assess the situation and hopefully agree with the President. We hoped he would testify at the Lend-Lease Hearings in our favor. Willkie came back and met with the President.

Mr. Willkie said he fully intends to support the Lend-Lease bill. When Mr. Willkie left, Franklin had a wide grin on his face.

He patted me on the head and said, "One down and one more to go!"

The following person Franklin had in mind was Joseph Kennedy. Mr. Kennedy was the former Ambassador to Great Britain and spread a rumor in Washington that Churchill was not a friend of America. Therefore, he was telling people in Congress to vote against the Lend-Lease Bill.

One morning I saw Mr. Kennedy walking into the President's bedroom. I thought it was rather strange to see someone like Mr. Kennedy speaking to Franklin while he was in bed eating breakfast. It was a perfect setup. It did not look official; the atmosphere was more relaxed. I jumped on the bed and listened very carefully. Mr. Kennedy resigned his post as Ambassador and complained that he was not treated well by the State Department. As Franklin nodded his head, he thought it was time to do something for Mr. Kennedy. The President lit his cigarette and started to talk about the good times they had together. He further said he was sorry about what happened in the State Dept. He would make it up to him.

"Let me tell you, Joe, once this bill passes, I will make sure the American people know how valuable your services have been to the country."

Franklin then started asking about Mr. Kennedy's children, especially the boys. They compared notes about their sons, especially Mr. Kennedy's son John.

When Mr. Kennedy left, Franklin said to me, "I am not sure if that was a home run, but it was a base hit!"

The Lend-Lease Hearings started with Wendell Willkie testifying for the bill. Next, Joseph Kennedy testified, and he changed his statement much to the surprise of his isolationist friends. He did not support the bill but was not opposed to it.

When he finished, Franklin, who was listening to the statement, said, "Wow, Fala, I thought for a minute we lost him."

The one person that the President could not depend on was Charles Lindbergh. He testified that passing this bill was one step away from democracy and one step towards war. After this, Roosevelt went on the attack again. This time he spoke with Harry Hopkins, who was still in London.

"Harry, let's get Winnie to help us out with this Lend-Lease debate."

Churchill agreed to make a speech. We were in a cabinet meeting when Mr. Churchill spoke about Europe turning into a brutal force under Hitler, and tyranny would be the law of the land.

We educated the public very successfully. The Lend-Lease approval rating was raised from 50 to 61%. The bill called HR1776 (Lend Lease) was submitted to Congress. While the debate was going on, the White House ordered a press conference. There I was, standing at the President's side, looking at all the reporters. They were asking questions, and the topic of getting involved in a European war came up. Many asked the President if he wanted to get involved. The expression on Franklin's face started to change.

He said, "These statements were not true and dastardly unpatriotic. It was the most rotten thing that has been said about my public life in my generation."

He said that building a military while lending our military products would make America strong.

The Lend-Lease bill HR1776 was passed. Congress would allow 7 billion dollars to make munitions for Great Britain. We all celebrated! That night the President gave a fireside chat to the American people. He spoke about sacrifice during these challenging times. Lower profits and higher taxes were to come.

The President gave me the job as First Dog to be the head of Barkers for Britain. The concept came from the British version of

Bundles for Britain. Americans were asked to donate food, clothing, and whatever they could spare to help our friends across the ocean. The program I was to start, Barkers for Britain, was along the same line. Dog owners would pay 50 cents for a membership. The member would join a local Barkers Chapter. Each dog was sent a tag they could proudly wear. All proceeds were given to Great Britain for the war effort. I was given tag #1 in a press conference provided by the White House. There were tons of reporters calling my name, whistling, and making silly noises to get my attention. The camera lights bothered my eyes, and it took a few hours to get back to normal.

During the press conference, I autographed certificates for new members. I would put a paw print to certify the dog's membership. I handled the press conference very well, let out a few barks, performed a few tricks, and became the darling of the White House. I learned to handle the press from watching Franklin. The ole Roosevelt charm; after all, I was a Roosevelt!

Barkers for Britain was a very successful program.

About 30,000 Barker memberships were issued in the United States between April and October 1941. We also had memberships abroad in Australia. The President of Bundles for Britain wrote me a letter saying you, the First Dog of the United States, are a leader of all-American canines. She thanked me for raising my loud bark for the courageous people of Great Britain. This letter was given to the President, who said I was a real pro!

"You handled the press better than most of the Senate! Good job, ole Boy."

I walked away, real proud, not knowing the best was yet to come.

Chapter 10

The Atlantic Conference – August 14, 1941

There were whispers about another fishing expedition. I enjoyed the last trip aboard the Tuscaloosa, and I was hoping to be invited. But then I heard the President say no one, not even my mother, must know about this trip! I did not understand why everything was such a secret.

Mr. Fields said, "Mr. President, your sons Elliot and Franklin have been ordered to the Augusta as you requested."

Wow, this is some fishing party! I played around the house when I saw Franklin getting ready to leave. He never mentioned to me about going on the trip. I started to whimper and sat beside him.

With pleasure in his voice, the President said, "Fala ole boy, you are coming with us! This trip is a man's trip, so get your ball, and let's get going!"

I will never forget how excited I was. It seemed everyone was going, even the President's doctor!

Our trip started with a train ride from Union Station in Washington, D.C., to New London, Connecticut. We then boarded a ship called the USS Potomac. This ship was Franklin's favorite. The Potomac was not very big, but it did the job. Everyone referred to this ship as the floating White House.

We sailed up the coastline towards Massachusetts. We made a stop and picked up some passengers. I met for the first time Princess Martha of Norway and her children. She was a friend of Franklin and was living in the United States. Nazi Germany invaded her country, and the whole family had to flee. Things in Europe were getting worse by the minute, and anyone who could afford to left. One of the children that I met was Prince Harald. He was about eight years old and adored animals. He was a ton of fun to play with. He told me how much he missed home and was unsure when he could go back. He told me how the Nazis were imposing their laws on the people of Norway. If you disagreed with them or were Jewish, you were sent away, never to be seen again. I wondered if Franklin knew about this.

It was time to move on. I sadly said my goodbyes to Harald. He told me that he would see me at the White House. It was such a shame; he was a Prince without a country.

On my journey, I saw the USS Augusta. We were sailing right next to each other when both ships parked parallel. Each dropped their anchors and a gangplank when they were side by side. This gangplank was very special because it had hand railings. It gave the President the freedom to walk independently. Franklin was determined. He walked slowly, concentrating on every step, and made it onto the ship. Standing on the other side of the vessel were the President's sons, Elliot and Franklin. All of the Roosevelt boys had joined the service, and both were on duty in the area. They had no idea the President was coming when they received orders to report to the Augusta. I never saw such a proud smile on Franklin's face when he saw his sons.

As I watched the Potomac sail away, I noticed a man waving at us who looked just like Franklin. He had the cigarette holder in his mouth and typical fishing gear. We all started to laugh, and the President said,

"He looks like me. That will shut them up."

A telegram said the weather was good, and fishing was going well. These telegrams were sent by Washington every day while we were on our trip. As the Augusta set sail, it started to get very windy and cold. We all went to the Admiral's quarters, where I was presented with a dog coat.

This coat was made especially for me. It was a sailor's coat and had a V for victory patch on the side. I wore this coat on many trips. I think I looked rather handsome wearing it around the ship.

There was not much to do because Franklin was meeting with his staff. So, I decided to go on deck and saw many other ships sailing with us. I counted six vessels, including the Tuscaloosa!

Little did I know the other ships were sweeping mines that Nazi Germany could have planted in the ocean.

As I walked on the deck, a steel cable was ready to unravel. I did not see the rope, and was dangerously close.

A sailor picked me up and saved my life. If the line broke or hit me, I could have been thrown into the water or badly injured. I could have been the first American casualty of the war! Instead, the President ordered a sailor to have "Fala Duty." The sailor never let me out of his sight and was a great companion.

The following day, it was time for deep-sea fishing. We all went in a small whaleboat, which the President piloted. I had on my sailor's coat, and I was nice and warm. Franklin had on an old sweatshirt with his floppy hat to protect him from the sun. That cigarette holder never left his lips. He caught this real ugly fish that no one could identify. We were to find out the name of the fish was a Dogfish! I looked at it and did not think it was so ugly after all. To me, it looked like a shark with no teeth. As a side note, I think catfish are ugly.

I saw another ship come through the fog the next day.

Franklin said, "There she is!"

As the ship got closer, we noticed that she was rather battered. The British battleship, the HMS Prince of Wales, sailed towards us. I was to learn this was one of her better ships! A man was waving and seemed rather excited to see us. I caught my first glimpse of Winston Churchill.

"He does look like Fiorello LaGuardia (The mayor of New York), doesn't he?" said Franklin.

I thought to myself, *He looks more like W.C. Fields.*

The President took the arm of Franklin Jr. and greeted Mr. Churchill. As Mr. Churchill walked down the gangplank, he was followed by a black and white cat. I kept my composure. The first thing I wanted to do was chase that darn cat back up the plank and get her back onto the Prince of Wales.

"Well, look, Fala, we have a First cat for you to play with," jokingly said the President.

I let out a sigh and a soft woof, but all I could do was watch that cat. Then, finally, both the President and the Prime Minister said it was about time to meet. When Mr. Churchill spoke, he sounded a little funny in how he pronounced his words.

I was introduced to Blackie the Cat. It was my duty to show her around the ship. I must say she was charming for a cat, kind of quiet and reserved. She would be my companion for the next few days. I taught Blackie the fine art of getting table scraps and doing tricks. She learned to get table scraps quite well, but she did not want to do tricks. I tried to explain to her the more tricks you do, the more food you get. She said it is beneath a cat to perform for her master. That is why you are a dog, and I am a cat. I started to respect Blackie; she was very wise and understood her position very well. I was also very proud of myself. I handled a situation that could have been a complete disaster into a learning experience. Humans have difficulty understanding each other and respecting each other's right to feel the way they want. When you get someone like Mr. Hitler, that promises everything to those who will follow him, then imprisons those who disagree, that is when wars start. It is far more complicated in the dog's world, yet it is the same in many ways. We are similar because both animals and humans want control of power and land. Blackie and I spent many hours talking about our differences and how different we were from Humans.

It was the Americans' turn to board the HMS Prince of Wales. Franklin was determined to walk the gangplank onto the Prince of Wales. His son was at his side, and his head held high as he walked. The President successfully boarded, and we were greeted by Royal Navy's band playing "Stars and Stripes Forever." Blackie showed me around the ship. I could not believe how beaten up the ship was. Blackie recounted the significant battle the Prince Of Wales was in with the great German Ship the Bismarck. Blackie told me how scary war was. All the explosions, noise, and fire. She did not think they would have survived. I never realized how brave she was.

The President brought onboard packages of fruit and food, which were distributed to each British sailor. The American sailors were also surprised when they opened gifts from the British.

On the last day together, we attended a religious service, and everyone was singing. Mr. Churchill as the representative of the United Kingdom, and Franklin Roosevelt, President of the United States, let everyone know their shared beliefs and that they would stick together through thick and thin. After Nazi Germany was defeated, they would want all nations to live in peace and for their citizens to be safe and live in freedom. When we started to part our ways, Mr. Churchill shook Franklin's hand and patted me on the head. I said goodbye to Blackie and told her to be safe.

Mr. Churchill said to the President. "That was a great hour to be alive."

Chapter 11

The Greer And a Sad Goodbye - September 9, 1941

The first time I heard of an attack on American forces was in September of 1941. I listened to the President talking on the phone; he was very annoyed. He summoned a few of his advisors and told them to come to the Oval Office.

"Well, friends, we have a problem. Today a German Submarine ship fired on one of our American destroyers. They knew it was an American ship! I will not stand for any aggression against our armed forces. I want to make a statement for Mr. Hitler and Mr. Mussolini (the Italian dictator) to hear."

I found out later the real story. Our ship, the USS Greer, was stalking a German Submarine. The Greer was accompanying a British plane that had attacked a German U boat. The Greer continued to pursue the German Sub. In response, the U-Boat fired back at the Greer. The ship's captain informed his superiors, then told the White House. The Greer lost contact with the submarine and continued to Iceland.

What the President failed to do was to tell his advisors the whole story. Instead, he intentionally left out a few essential parts to gain support for Germany and Italy's upcoming conflict.

A phone call then came into the Oval office. The President's face turned ash white as he was talking.

He said softly, "I will be home as soon as possible."

All appointments were canceled, and the President sent a telegram to his mother informing her he would be coming home. Before I knew it, we were all on the train headed for Hyde Park.

When we returned home, the President's mother, Sara, was gravely ill. The phone call was from Eleanor, who felt the end for Sara was near. She wanted Franklin to come home and spend some time with his mother. Sara had been at their home at Campobello, Maine, when her health started to decline. Finally, the doctors decided that she should return to Hyde Park. Sara was such a stubborn woman who wanted to prove to her staff that she did not need to be carried down the stairs. It took all her strength to do so, and Sara left Campobello for the last time.

When she returned home, Eleanor noticed that Sara's breathing was labored. I know Eleanor was praying that Franklin would get home in time. Sara received the telegram and had a look of sheer delight on her face. Sara always made it a point to look her best when Franklin came home.

Unfortunately, Sara was too weak to go downstairs to greet him upon our arrival. She was lying in her room on a chaise lounge chair. Franklin rolled his wheelchair to her, kissed her on the cheek, and held her hand. Sara said she was thinking about the good times they had. He was constantly in her thoughts and always in her heart. I knew Franklin was holding back the tears.

Later in the day, Sara seemed to be getting better. The color on her face returned, and she wanted to hear all the latest Washington gossip. He told her about Lend Lease and the Greer Incident. She joined the family for dinner.

Eleanor kept looking at Franklin with great concern. In the evening, as she was lying in her bed, Sara lapsed into a coma. Franklin stayed with her throughout the night and did not sleep a wink. With her son by her side, Sara Roosevelt died by the following day. Not more than five minutes after her death, the largest tree on the property fell. Franklin was so shaken by the news that he went out to look at the tree. A geologist told the Boss that trees falling in Dutchess County in New York were very common because of the terrain. I knew Franklin thought otherwise.

Sara's funeral was very simple and took place in the library. The service was at Saint James Church which was not far from Springwood.

Sara's body was buried in the cemetery in the churchyard. I heard that the President could not look at the grave. Instead, he stood by his vehicle, holding on with one hand, and did not show any emotion.

We learned that Sara died of a blood clot in her lung. It comforted me that she died happy with her loving son next to her. The whole family mourned.

The next day, the President and his secretary Grace Tully started to go through Sara's papers. A box was found in the closet. Franklin opened the box and said, "Oh God." The box contained Franklin's toys, a lock of his hair, and his christening dress. He asked Grace to leave, and the tears rolled down his face. I sat next to him and watched all those built-up emotions come out. He was so sad.

I never wrote too much about Sara, but she was one of my favorites. She was a very warm person, generous, and loved to control her son. She was always concerned if Franklin was wearing a hat or if his throat was covered when it was cold. Everyone called her Grandma except to her face. I do not think she approved of his Presidency. Sara did not always agree with Franklin regarding politics, was very vocal about her opinion, and did not care who was around. Sara always carried herself like she was the first lady, bragged proudly about her son, and always let everyone know whose mother she was. Sara never liked all the fanfare whenever the President came to Hyde Park. She was very critical of the Secret Service. One time we were in the rose garden, she waited for all the Secret Service to leave; she then commented to me,

"Don't these people believe in picking up their cigarette butts?"

She proceeded to clean up their mess while commenting that they all looked like a bunch of gangsters.

There was one story that Franklin loved to tell about his mother. One of Sara's friends was traveling in Europe and could not return because of the war. Sara spoke to Franklin about the situation and wanted him to send a battleship to pick up her friend. She could not understand why Franklin could not do this.

Sara then said, "Then what are you, President, for?"

The same week Eleanor's brother Hall collapsed in his home. Hall was rushed to the hospital and soon afterward died.

The President and I headed back to Washington, and we both were in a solemn mood. Things in Europe were deteriorating day by day. The President prepared his speech about the Greer situation with the American people.

The President had to get back to work as soon as possible.

He was so sad about his mother and Hall, but the Greer Incident was an issue that demanded immediate attention. The President had to address the country as soon as possible.

The President made the speech from the White House basement. Franklin wore a black armband in remembrance of his mother. He would touch the armband as if he was asking Sara for strength. He told Hitler and Mussolini that America would not stand for any unprovoked attacks in his speech. The waterways of the Atlantic should be made safe. The American Navy would shoot any German or Italian vessel that entered these protective waters. A poll showed that 62% of the American people supported the President.

Capitol Hill seemed to have changed overnight. I felt not telling the whole story of the Greer incident was not fair. Deception is never a good thing, and I hoped Franklin never did that again.

The end came for Hall on September 25, 1941. Eleanor felt that she had lost not only a brother but a child. I heard her say that Mother Roosevelt lived eighty-Six years and had a full life with many experiences. Poor Hall was only fifty- one year old. Eleanor felt he could have done much more with his life. It was a terrible loss. The night he died, Eleanor took out photographs of Hall and a letter he had written her. Looking at all of this made her so unhappy. She lit a fire and threw the letter into the flames. I guess she was destroying all the pain. She felt numb with sorrow and regret. Franklin entered that room and saw what she had done. Even though Franklin and Eleanor had their moments, I believe that he truly loved her and understood her pain. He held her hand, and both watched the fire.

Chapter 12

Pearl Harbor - December 7, 1941

Today started like any other day. I woke up, stretched, and ran downstairs to get some food. My bowl was ready to be filled. Everyone seemed to be happy.

Things can change so fast, like in a blink of an eye. One minute you hear laughter. The next, the silence could be deafening.

We were down in Warm Springs visiting Missy, who was ill and recuperating from a stroke. Franklin thought it would be an excellent time to visit and cheer her up.

The boss got a phone call from Washington. The look on his face told me something was wrong. He talked with Cordell Hall, his Secretary of State, on the phone. They were discussing the United States Relationship with the Empire of Japan.

Japan had invaded Indochina, trying to expand its Empire. As a result, the United States instituted sanctions against Japan by cutting off its ability to get oil and scrap metal. The Japanese needed these materials for their war effort. The President knew Japan was unhappy about the embargo and sent their ambassadors to negotiate with the United States.

Concerned, the President said, "I think they are going to retaliate and hit us in either Thailand, the Philippines, or Malaya. Maybe the negotiations will go well. That will be one less thing for us to worry about."

Soon afterward, Franklin read intelligence that the Japanese fleet was traveling south of Japan.

The President said, "I'm on my way."

We packed our bags and returned to the White House.

On the train, Franklin was very quiet. He had a concerned look on his face. He was deep in thought, trying to lay out his options, not knowing what was coming next. When we arrived at the White House, the phone rang. It was about 7:30 at night. Franklin picked up the phone, and his face turned a pale white.

He said, "My God, No!"

He kept repeating himself when his head turned down in disbelief. He summoned his Cabinet for a prompt meeting.

He was calm, did not greet anyone as he usually did. His voice was low yet stern.

"Today, our naval base at Pearl Harbor was attacked by the Empire of Japan. There were three waves of attacks. As far as I know, eight battleships, three destroyers, and three light cruisers are gone."

Everyone had a look of disbelief on their faces.

Meanwhile, the intelligence was still coming in. Franklin could not even imagine the loss of life that had just happened.

Eleanor stopped by the office and sensed that something was wrong. The phones were ringing off the hook, and people were running around. Eleanor returned to her office and waited to hear from the President. Soon afterward, a note summoned her to see the President as quickly as possible.

Eleanor was utterly stunned. Franklin told her to contact their daughter Ana and have her move to the east coast.

"We are not sure if their next target will be the west coast. Please contact the boys, tell them to come to the White House as soon as possible," said the President

The phone rang again with more terrible news. The ships were docked close together, side by side, and were easy targets for the Japanese bombers. The Navy took a big hit, but not all of our fleet was anchored at Pearl Harbor.

Franklin took this attack very hard. As the former Assistant Secretary of the Navy under President Woodrow Wilson, the Navy was dear to his heart.

During his meeting with his Cabinet, the President said, "I must address a joint session of Congress."

The President started to write his speech. Grace Tully, his secretary, entered the room and started taking dictation as the President spoke. Franklin chose his words very carefully. December 7, 1941, is A day that will live in world history. He had to choose the right words to make it effective as possible. When the President completed writing, he gave the speech to Grace to type. He knew a rewrite was necessary.

Franklin was in deep thought for several minutes.

He said to Eleanor, "There is something about this first sentence I want to change.

With his hand rubbing the side of his head, the pencil made its mark. He crossed out world history and replaced it.

"December 7, 1941, a day that will live in infamy.".

He read it out loud, and I barked my approval.

"You like this ole boy? I think we have it!

A joint session of Congress was assembled and was waiting for the President's speech. Stern, in his voice, the President, stood on the podium and declared war on the Empire of Japan. Congress voted and overwhelmingly voted in favor of the war declaration

When the President came home, he said to Eleanor, "Now it's time for me to talk to the American people."

This fireside chat was the first since the Pearl Harbor. attack The President talked to the American people as their friend, leader, and advisor. He told them no matter how dark things seemed, victory was bound to come.

He compared this war to the Revolution and the difficulties that General Washington faced. Nevertheless, the General stood the course, and the darkness turned to light, and soon a new country was created.

Before the Fireside chat began, the White House instructed Americans to purchase a world map. The day before the President was to speak, he said,

"I am going to speak of places you may have never heard," said the President in a calm voice.

He was teaching and letting the public know what he could without letting any secret intelligence out. A geography lesson made the people understand and trust his judgment.

The chat was successful as he prepared Americans for the future of our country. Young men and women willingly signed up to defend America. Some were drafted, and those too young to enlist lied about their age and signed up anyway.

The American spirit touched Mr. Roosevelt's heart. I knew with the determination of the American people; we would win this war!

Chapter 13

Christmas! - December 22, 1941

It's getting close to Christmas! The smells of fresh-baked cakes and cookies came from the White House kitchen.

Many of the staff members decorated the White House with Christmas trees with lights and garland. This Christmas was quite different. There were no Christmas carols, no song of joy; the atmosphere was somber. On the fireplace, there were two stockings—one for my friend Diana Hopkins, and one for me. My stocking was given to me by Eleanor, filled with rubber toys and treats. There were not many family members at home. All the Roosevelt boys joined the armed services while Ana was still on the west coast.

A lot of people died at Pearl Harbor. The attack killed 2,403 people. The nation was not ready to have a Merry Christmas.

A special visitor is coming today. It was supposed to be a secret, but I knew who it was. The President was keeping the secret; not even Eleanor knew. But when she found out, oh boy, she was fuming!

"How am I going to get the White house ready? Where will he sleep? Are the rooms ready? Mrs. Nesbitt is not even in the White house!"

The President left the White House to meet the special guest at about 6:00. Once again, I could not go, but I made sure I was there when the cars pulled up.

I stood at attention when the cars arrived. Stepping out was Mr. Winston Churchill. He had a long black coat, cigar in his mouth. When he entered the house, he asked where the brandy was, so typical of Winston.

Eleanor said to him, "I want to show you your room so you can get settled. Then, I will have one of the staff come for you so we can have tea."

He grunted and smiled at Eleanor.

Mr. Fields took Mr. Churchill to the Lincoln bedroom. He was getting the grand treatment! The Lincoln bedroom was the nicest room in the house. As Winston walked into the room and sat on the bed, and in a Goldilocks style, he said, "This will not do; the bed is too hard."

He walked through the hallways going in and out of each room. He sat on each bed until he found a bed to his liking. He chose the Rose Room; He sat on the bed and said, this is just right. He turned his head and saw me and said,

"Fala ole boy, how is my favorite Scotsman doing today?"

He petted my head and proceeded to look around the room while his valet started putting his luggage away.

I then accompanied Winston down the stairs to meet the President.

Franklin said, "Winnie, ole boy, how are you?"

Mr. Churchill answered back, "The better question is, how are you?" First, tell me about Pearl Harbor."

The President then said, "How about a few before dinner?"

Eleanor had asked Mr. Fields for tea before dinner, but I know Winston wanted something more potent.

Much to Franklin's delight, Mrs. Nesbit was unable to cook dinner that night, so Mr. Fields oversaw the dinner. They had baked chicken, vegetables, and ice cream. I saw a few hands under the table with some scraps for me.

The President said this chicken was delicious and had no broccoli!

"My compliments to the cook!" the President said.

After dinner, Winston and Franklin went to the Oval Office for a brandy and a cigar.

I was taking notice that Mr. Churchill loved his brandy. He had a blue jumpsuit on and looked like a combination of a sea captain and a kewpie doll. I always found him quite humorous, intelligent, and good with his words.

Mr. Churchill had several requests from the staff during his stay. A tumbler of sherry in the morning before breakfast, a 90-year-old brandy before he went to sleep.

Food was secondary. Mr. Fields was writing down everything so fast.

Then Mr. Churchill turned to me and said," Fala ole boy, no barking until after 11:00 am!"

Mr. Churchill met with the President in the Oval Office.

Both leaders discussed the current situation in Europe.

"We will discuss the Europe first strategy, right?" said Churchill nervously.

Winston's greatest fear was that the United States would focus on Japan and leave England to fight Germany.

Franklin then told him that Adolf Hitler had made the decision. Hitler declared war on the United States; now we have a two-front war.

The next day, The Prime Minister gave a great speech before congress. When he returned to the White House, I walked up to Winston's room. Mr. Churchill was trying to open a window for some fresh air. He had a disturbed look on his face; and made a call for a Doctor. Mr. Churchill told the doctor that he had chest pain radiating down the left side of his arm. The doctor checked him and told him everything was fine. The doctor advised Mr. Churchill he was doing too much and to get some rest. Harry Hopkins came into the room, overhearing what had transpired. I overheard the doctor tell someone over the phone that Mr. Churchill may have suffered a heart attack. Harry told the doctor that he would not say a word. Mr. Hopkins kept that secret until Mr. Churchill died many years later. I think if his doctor had told Mr. Churchill that he had a heart attack, it would have been a disaster for himself and Great Britain.

Christmas day came and went. I did enjoy the treats and my new rubber ball. At dinner the next day, Franklin made a toast.

"To the Common cause!"

When Winston was leaving, I overheard him say, meeting Franklin

Roosevelt was like opening your first bottle of champagne; knowing him was like drinking it.

One of the first things I learned was performing tricks for the President.

Photo Credit: The Franklin Roosevelt Presidential Library

Working hard with the President at the White House.

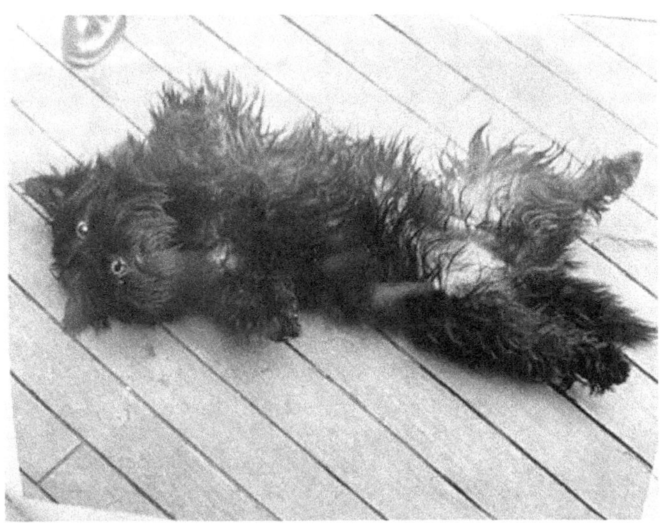

Lying on the deck if the USS Tuscaloosa - Photo Credit: The Franklin Roosevelt Presidential Library

The Atlantic Conference - I am sitting at the President's feet.

The Informer.- Photo Credit: The Franklin Roosevelt Presidential Library

I learned how to handle the press from the boss.

My family. I am first, then Meggie, Peggie, and Buttons. Photo Credit: The Franklin
Roosevelt Presidential Library

I really loved the Christmas cards from all my fans. Photo Credit: Barbara Guerriero
Flites

Sympathy cards from all over the country. These really comforted me when the President died - Photo Credit: Barbara Guerriero-Flites

Chapter 14

The Girls and a Boy - January 15, 1942

Franklin was a very complicated person. He had many friends, but no one knew his inner feelings. When meetings occurred with his staff, I noticed that the President always agreed with everybody with a smile. When they left, he would take his time and decide what he should do.

Sometimes the Boss would play people against each other. He would always be in the eye of the storm when it came to politics.

His relationship with women was also very different. He had several women in his life that he respected and loved. However, most were just for companionship.

Franklin had an affair with Eleanor's secretary, Lucy Mercer, before he came down with polio. He was willing to give everything up for her. When Franklin spoke to his mother about divorcing Eleanor, Sara immediately rejected the idea. If he decided to go against her wishes, Franklin would be written out of the Roosevelt will and inheritance.

Society did not approve divorce in those days. Eleanor was crushed by the affair and always kept it in the back of her mind.

Lucy Mercer, I feel, was the love of Franklin's life. She was beautiful, elegant, and refined. She married a man much older than her after the affair. When her husband fell ill, Franklin and Lucy continued to see each other. Lucy had a confidential name for when she tried to contact the President. The President's aides knew that if Mrs. Paul Johnson phoned, the call would be put through no matter the meeting or what crisis he was involved with.

Missy Le hand was the President's secretary for many years. She was dependable and was his confidant. He loved a good laugh, and so did Missy. I heard Missy tell people that no one is as close to the President as she was. After suffering several strokes, the President insisted that Missy goes to Warm Springs for her rehabilitation. I knew when Franklin was troubled, but he never showed his feelings. I think he had difficulty expressing emotion when it came to the physical illnesses of a loved one. Their friendship was so important that the President had willed half of his estate to Missy. Franklin said that she would need to be cared for with her illness, just as she took care of me. Unfortunately, Missy died before Franklin.

Franklin's cousin Polly was a relation on the Delano side. Her real name was Laura, but I am not sure about the origins of her name. Polly was very eccentric. You never knew day to day what color her hair would be. Somedays, it was purple; other days, it was mauve. She painted a widow's peak on her forehead every day. She wore a lot of jewelry which always clacked together whenever she moved. She was very outspoken, vibrant, and fun to be around. She loved dogs and bred Irish Setters and Dachshunds. She also judged dog shows. I know Franklin enjoyed her company.

His cousin Margaret Suckley was also a very close companion. They wrote to each other constantly. When Franklin was in Washington or Hyde Park, Margaret made sure they were in contact. Under Margaret's bed, there were boxes of letters, which she kept. She would read them repeatedly to remember the good times they shared. They loved each other's company. They talked many hours into the night about life and family.

Franklin designed a house in the middle of nowhere in Hyde Park on top of a mountain. It was his getaway place. It was a small house with a beautiful porch with nothing but trees in front of it. The name of the house was Top Cottage. When Missy, Polly, and Margaret were getting in the car, they always knew when they were going to Top Cottage.

Franklin would take the car and drive through roads that were not well-traveled. It was still a lot of fun trying to lose the Secret Service. The ride was very bumpy, and I almost fell out of the car many times. They would all be laughing, singing, and just having a great time. Franklin needed this to ease his mind from the pressures of the Presidency and his disability. Those days were lots of fun and were the best days of my life.

I wanted to leave Eleanor for last, not because I felt less about her. On the contrary, she was probably the most important person in my life, next to Franklin. I loved her dearly.

The affair with Lucy Mercer hit Eleanor hard. The man she loved betrayed her.

When Franklin came down with polio, Eleanor felt obligated to take care of him; He was the father of their five children. She did not want the family to be separated or impacted by a divorce. Franklin needed her, and Eleanor needed him. So, she supported him in purchasing Warm Springs, while his mother felt this confirmed his disability.

Eleanor told him about the racial laws in Georgia and how she found them very disturbing. She soon after started to develop her voice outside of her marriage. She became involved with Women's Clubs in Hyde Park, giving speeches and getting politically involved. When Franklin became President, Eleanor was the first to have her own press conferences and became the New Deal's driving force. She traveled all over the United States, created awareness, and gave hope to the American people. As First Lady, she became his legs and traveled places he could not. Eleanor gave him reports about her thoughts and experiences. As a result, Eleanor's relationship with the President changed from a wife and mother to a political partner. There was genuine love there, don't get me wrong. but it was a different type of love not even I could explain.

Eleanor was a passionate, loving person. She was strong and set new boundaries for all women.

I do have to admit; she made the best scrambled eggs!

Chapter 15

Executive Order 9066 - February 19, 1942

Most Presidents have a dark period. Decisions they made, which would stain their legacy. Executive Order 9066 was President Roosevelt's. The purpose of this order was to place Japanese American citizens into internment camps. They relocated private citizens regardless of age or gender.

President Roosevelt's decision was based on Congress's pressure and the American people's hysteria after Pearl Harbor. Even though most Americans supported it, I feel this was a horrible decision.

After Pearl Harbor, Asian Americans were attacked by gangs for revenge after the bombing of Pearl Harbor.

Newspapers ran articles and cartoons depicting the Japanese as animals with stereotyped features. Many citizens wrote to the President and told him of the hatred, rage, and anger towards the Japanese people.

The FBI conducted raids into Japanese homes, primarily community, and religious leaders. These officers had no warrants. The FBI conducted the searches, and no intelligence was ever found. The houses raided were the homes of loyal citizens of the United States. Japanese Americans' assets were frozen, fishing boats were impounded, and shops were forced to close per the government's order.

The President had many meetings after Pearl Harbor to discuss keeping America safe. However, he was under pressure after the public and their representatives' outcries.

That is when Executive Order 9066 was created. The order called for every person of Japanese descent, citizen or not, men, women, and children, to be relocated into internment camps. Most of these Japanese citizens lived on the west coast.

It was decided that camps were in California, Washington, Arizona, and Oregon. The government told each family to pack what they could, and they should take

$100.00 out of the bank for expenses. All Japanese families were given dates and times to arrive at the train station with all of their belongings.

When they arrived at the camp, they found the conditions almost uninhabitable. Houses were shacks with walls made of wood. Significant gaps in between each plank exposed the outdoor elements. There was no privacy for using toilets or bathing. There were not enough facilities for everyone, and the lines were very long.

One could get a job inside the camp, but the government insisted that no one be paid more than an Army Private.

There were schools, farming, and odd jobs around the base. The people tried to make the best of a bad situation by making the camp look like home.

Most families were housed together in one barrack. They ate, worked, played, and socialized as a family, all of this being surrounded by barbed wire and guard towers.

When Eleanor found out about the internment camps, she immediately went to the Presidents office. She was given a file with newspaper clippings about what was going on.

"Franklin, did you approve of this?"

Eleanor threw the file on his desk.

"Do you realize what you have done? You put American Citizens in a camp for being Japanese. They committed no crime. Some of these people have signed up for military service. How can you even think to imprison them!"

Franklin had no answer. She stormed out of the room and went to her office. The First Lady asked her secretary to book a flight to the Gila River Internment Camp in Phoenix, Arizona. When Eleanor arrived at the camp, she could not believe her eyes. She wrote in her report that she certainly would not live there. The conditions are terrible. I am impressed with the character and perseverance of the inmates to make life as normal as possible.

In her report, she included a picture of a closed Japanese business with a sign on the door saying,

"I am an American." She also said it was her duty to undo a mistake. We have no common race in this country but a common ideal we are loyal to.

When FDR read her report, he was bothered by what he saw. He immediately explored releasing some detainees with work permits to leave the camps. About one-third of all detainees were soon released.

The President then conferred with his staff to discuss how to confront the hysteria without adding more.

The Supreme Court heard arguments about the internment camps and decided the order was unconstitutional. However, the President released all detainees one day before the Supreme Court announced its decision. Our nation experienced the end of an unfortunate chapter in our history and the stain on Roosevelt's legacy. I am not quite sure if Franklin was comfortable with this decision from the start. I think the President gave in to the hysteria and racist attitudes of the citizens and Congress. I guess you can say it was a political decision. Franklin should have listened to his better angels and not given in to hysteria.

Franklin Delano Roosevelt was not a good President; he was a great President, yet this stain on his Presidency will always remain.

Chapter 16

Home Front, The War, and Willie - May 1, 1942

The morale of the country was low after the attack on Pearl Harbor. There was very little good news coming from the Pacific. One horrible report after another. Songs on the radio were about the war. A girl missing a sweetheart, Tommy Dorsey, Glen Miller was always playing in the White House. One of my favorites was "Don't sit under the Apple Tree" by the Andrew Sisters. The radio provided news so people could be informed with the latest information. If you wanted to see newsreels, movie houses provided war films before the latest feature film.

The President was on the phone talking about how to improve the country's morale.

"We need to make a bold move; something, anything, no matter how small it is. Let's put ourselves on the offensive." He was talking to Chester Nimitz, Commander of the Pacific Theater. The plan was to bomb Japan. We had to get the planes as close as possible to the Japanese coast. But how could we do this? The United States had aircraft carriers in the Pacific. The plan was to load the aircraft with bombs and get as close to Japan as possible. The goal was to drop bombs and to return safely. The plan sounded easy, but it was not. One problem was the amount of fuel it would take to fly a plane to Japan and back without running out of gas. The second was the weight of the bombs on the aircraft. The planes would require more space for take-off and landing.

These planes were on aircraft carriers, and if they missed their mark, they would crash into the sea.

"We will see what we could work out. Mr. President. "said Admiral

Nimitz.

After much preparation and practice, the planes boarded the USS Hornet. The Japanese navy did not detect the USS Hornet, which was 600 miles from the coast of Japan. Naval command decided Lieutenant Colonel James Doolittle would be in charge of this mission and all the aircraft involved.

The Doolittle Raid, as it became known, had minimal impact on Japan. The casualties were light, but the morale in the United States soared. Lieutenant Colonel Doolittle survived even though his plane crashed in China. He thought he would be court marshaled because he felt the mission failed. Instead, Lieutenant Doolittle was awarded the Presidential Congressional Medal of Honor. Many of the other pilots were taken prisoner and did not survive.

Nevertheless, this daring mission would lead to the turning point of the Pacific war, The Battle of Midway.

Two of Franklin's sons were awarded medals for their bravery during the war. It never ceases to amaze me the courage of the men and women who served during this difficult time.

Many Generals came to the White House to visit the President. I sat in many meetings in various places, just listening.

My favorite General was George Patton. He was stern, harsh, and his men loved him. General Patton had the ultimate respect for his troops, especially the wounded. He would not put up with anything out of line or what he thought was cowardice. The General was a great speaker and inspired his troops. Patton's men love his blunt nature and curses during speeches, as his superiors looked in horror as he spoke. General Patton graduated from West Point and served during World War I. The General's specialty was tank warfare.

Patton had an English Bulldog by his side named Willie.

The General had a soft spot for him. I found out he was named after William the Conqueror. Willie was one dog that did not live up to his name. Willie was shy and scared of everything. He would hide between the General's legs and whimper. I am not sure if Willie was scared of the

General or the war. He was by Patton's side until the General's untimely death.

Willie and I spent many hours playing and hunting for whatever we could. He seemed at ease when he was with me, but Willie would tense up and run to Patton's side when the General called him. I liked Willie and wished him well when he left. I found out later Willie was involved in the European part of the war. He was on the front lines during many battles. Now I know why Willie was so nervous.

The President met with General Patton many times.

Franklin would often say you always knew what the General was thinking. During their meetings, I heard Franklin laugh and shake his head. Poor Willie would be under the table, either shaking or staring at me. I think he was a timid soul behind a tough exterior. General Patton knew about Willie's anxiety and would just shake his head and say, "imagine me with such a dog."

The other General I liked was Dwight Eisenhower. Like General Patton, they both graduated from West Point. Even though they went to the same school, the two could not have been any different. General Eisenhower was born in Kansas. He was of Pennsylvania Dutch heritage. His family disapproved of his career in the military because they were against the war in any form. The General was a great painter and was a sharp player of cards. He also enjoyed playing golf. President Roosevelt could not play golf, so they decided that poker was the sport, and both enjoyed it immensely.

Late nights after dinner and brandy in the oval office, the President would ask certain guests to report to the White House basement. The guests were members of the Cuff Links Club. They would play poker well into the night. They were placing wagers, and sounds of laughter and the smell of cigars went into the wee hours of the morning.

These were fun times at the White House. Even though the war was waging on, soldiers were dying, and battles were either won or lost. The President needed times like this to relieve the stress.

Chapter 17

The Invasion of North Africa - November 13, 1942

The President had a little secret cabin not far from the White House. It was Franklin's getaway from all the stress of Washington. He named it Shangri la; it would be later named Camp David. I noticed the President was very nervous and stressed. He had advisers around him, but he was preoccupied. The focus of the war would turn from the Pacific to Europe. When Winston Churchill was in Washington during the holidays, he suggested that the United States and Great Brittan's next move was to attack North Africa which was under Nazi control. Once done, they will go through Sicily, then to the Italian mainland, and then into Germany.

Mr. Churchill said, "We will attack through the "belly of the beast."

The other ally was Russia, headed by Joseph Stalin. Russia was very desperate and had over a million people dead after the battle of Leningrad. Marshall Stalin wanted the Allies to attack France and make their way to meet the Russians in Germany.

Franklin heard all sides. He listened to his advisors, his allies and decided to invade North Africa. General Eisenhower would lead the operation.

Now the time was getting near to when the invasion would take place. The amount of equipment that had to be brought over to the North African coast was tremendous. They brought tanks, jeeps, weapons, ammunition, and ships. Each soldier was responsible for carrying up to 180 pounds of supplies. The men could hardly move, let alone run onto the shore against heavy fire. The United States saw serious action for the first time. The name of this invasion was called Operation Torch

The phone rang, Grace Tully answered the phone. She gave the phone directly to the President.

"Thank God, Thank God!" the President said joyfully, with a massive smile on his face, Franklin said, "We have landed in North Africa; causalities are low. We have struck back."

Soon afterward, Franklin broadcasted a message to the people of North Africa.

"We came among you to defeat and rout your enemies. Have faith in our words. We do not want to cause you harm."

As time went by, the news of the invasion was excellent.

Morocco, Algeria, and Tunisia were in Allied hands. The German and Italian forces were in full retreat!

Eleanor was in Great Brittan and reported the victories. People were cheering, posting banners on the docks; "God bless our Men!"

Eleanor called Franklin and told him about the report. He listened with a smile on his face. "I want you home," he told her." As soon as possible,"

Eleanor was never one to just sit home. She went to New York and Philadelphia to attend rallies to support various social programs that supported the war effort. Everyone was busy with one task or another. We are all just trying to save the United States and save the world.

Chapter 18

No Words - December 31, 1942

Eleanor was off to New York to attend a day of mourning sponsored by the Jewish leaders. The purpose of this meeting was to make people aware of the situation of the European Jews. The news from all over Europe was terrifying. Jewish people were being forced out of their homes and transported to concentration camps in the east.

Once they arrived, it would be determined by the Nazis if they were to be forced into slave labor. We did not know what happened to those who could not work. The Nazis felt the Jews were the source of all the world's problems and were inferior to the Germans. We heard about a conference held by Nazi officials that all Jewish people throughout Europe should be eliminated.

The first time Eleanor heard of this, she could not believe her ears. The following day, she opened the New York Times, a usual ritual with her morning coffee. As she read it, her face had a look of terror. The article said that 2/3 of the Jewish population had been killed in Europe. Shortly afterward, she contacted Rabbi Stephan Wise. Eleanor told him about the article and asked if he knew anything. Much to her surprise, he told her of a document called the Reigner Report. This report confirmed there were as many as 20 concentration camps throughout Europe. The camp's sole purpose was to kill and exterminate Europe's Jewish population.

Jewish leaders were terrified. They asked to have a conference with the President to inform him of this situation. Unless the allies took some sort of action, Hitler would kill every Jewish person in Europe. Later that month, the conference with Rabbi Wise and Jewish leaders took place. Intelligence received by the President did mention that Jews were being transported eastward to labor camps. However, the State Department would not confirm anything about the mass killings for quite some time.

The President assured everyone that the United States would do everything in its power to be of service to the Jewish people. Little did he know he would face opposition.

The President tried to get a bill passed to open the gates for Jewish immigration. Unfortunately, the bill had no chance with the conservative Congress that was primarily antisemitic. As the war raged on, this situation worsened by the day.

Most people surrounding the President did not believe what the intelligence was saying. Many government officials just shrugged their shoulders and wanted solid proof before they would believe it. Franklin had a look on his face that told me he was very disturbed. In the back of his mind, I know he was trying to figure out his next move. The President felt the best way to stop the atrocities was to defeat the Nazis and win the war. I guess it was the best he could do. He was walking on a tight rope, trying to keep the support for the war going and getting Congress to go along with him. I only had wished the world could have gotten together and do something to help these poor people.

Chapter 19

Casablanca - January 28, 1943

"We are off for a grand adventure!" said the President with an excited look. You know I love to travel on the open seas! You are coming with me, Fala!

I could not help but wonder where on earth we were going. My bags were packed, I jumped in the car, and off we went. I found out that we were going to Morocco! One of the most beautiful countries in North Africa. We were to meet with Winston Churchill to discuss the war.

Security was tight. The Germans were trying to find out where the conference was taking place. When the Nazis found out that the location was Casablanca, their intelligence thought it translated as the White House, so the Germans thought the meeting was held in Washington. I got a good laugh at this, and so did Franklin. The group that thinks they were so superior to everyone else has faulty intelligence.

When we arrived in Morocco, we approached the hotel, and I saw a white building with beautiful palm trees. Further down the road, I saw barbed wire, which the Army put up to keep us locked in and safe. From a distance, I saw General Patton walking towards us. The General saluted and shook the President's hand. Willie was there, scared as ever. I gave him a look that everything was going to be ok.

"I hear the Desert Fox is a great admirer of yours, George!" said the President with a smile on his face.

The desert fox, General Irwin Rommel, was one of Nazi Germany's most outstanding leaders. General Patton started to laugh and told the Boss that his Third Battalion had surrounded the hotel, and it was an honor to be of service.

Security was tight all over the place. The Army provided food tasters who tasted every bit of food. Even my dog food was tested.

German troops were rationed to a few slices of bread a day, and many were dying of starvation at this point in the war. It would not be long before the Germans would surrender North Africa, but that was a long way ahead.

Mr. Churchill and the President discussed the next course of action. Both were under tremendous pressure from Marshall Stalin to open a front by invading France. Mr.

Stalin stated that the Soviet Union suffered more losses than Great Britain and the United States combined. They were not sure how long they could hang on.

The decision was made. The United States and Great Britain's joint Allied forces would continue the invasion into Sicily and the Italian mainland.

In the meeting, General Patton stood up and loudly said, "Give me the whole damn thing! I'll have my boys march right to the German Reichstag!

"Well, George, it looks like it's time to go to work!" said the President.

Little did General Patton know he would be sharing the duty with British General Bernard Montgomery. There are books written about that rivalry.

The next day we set off to Rabat, which was about 85 miles away, to visit the troops. General Patton and Willie were in the car in front of us. They so were honored to escort and protect us. The General would stand up in his car while he was being driven. He was directing the caravan like he was conducting an orchestra. I can tell you he was quite a character.

When we got to Rabat, we had lunch and then got ready to inspect the troops. The Ninth Infantry stood at attention, and we drove by in our car. I have to say they were impressive. All the men stood in line like wooden soldiers.

The President overheard one of the soldiers say, "Wow, it's the old man himself."

We all shook our heads and smiled, and continued our way. Finally, we stopped at a cemetery for our fallen soldiers and laid wreaths on the graves. It was such a sad sight. We all must remember with all the glory that comes with our freedom, and there is an unthinkable loss we should never forget.

We returned to the villa and had dinner with Mr.

Churchill and the Sultan of Morocco. The wonderful smells of spices were in the air. The Sultan gave Franklin beautiful gifts, such as a gold dagger and a tiara for the First Lady. My first thought; I could not imagine Eleanor in a tiara. I am sure the idea entered Franklin's mind also.

General Patton said. "This looks like something from the Bible. They are a wonderful people, and their troops are to be admired."

Winston Churchill sat across from us and was very quiet. When General Patton asked what was wrong, the President said, "Muslim tradition forbids the use of Alcohol. He will be better once he goes to his room."

We all looked at each other with smiles on our faces.

We were sitting out on the lawn of the hotel. The sky was blue, the sun was shining, and the temperature was just right. I know Franklin was pleased and decided to announce that the allies would not take anything less but an unconditional surrender. The press was in attendance, and I am sure Mr.

Hitler would hear about this very soon. The face of Mr. Churchill was one to remember. He had a worried yet surprised look. I don't think the Boss discussed the unconditional surrender with him.

"It gives us the upper hand. We are telling Germany and Italy that you are losing the war." said the President sternly

"I do have to say that came as a bit of a surprise. Don't you think this would make the Germans and the Italians fight harder?" said Winston.

"We set the terms of the war; we will win the war," said Franklin.

With our trip soon coming to an end, we all decided to visit the city of Marrakesh. Mr. Churchill insisted that we spend two days there.

"I want to be with you when the sun sets on the Atlas Mountains," said Winston.

Franklin did not need any excuse to stay. We got into the car and started to drive to the mountains. There was a villa there, and Mr. Churchill made all the arrangements. What a beautiful place, I thought. Waterfalls, palm trees, and pools. Just up Franklin's alley!

Inside the villa was a tower, which was six stories high. "I want to see the sunset from the tower with you," said Winston.

Franklin looked at Winston with a puzzled look.

"Winston, you know my position. How could I ever get up there?"

Winston chuckled and said, isn't that what the secret service is for?"

We had many strong secret service agents. My favorite was Mike Early. He reminded me of a movie star. The way he wore his hat and his whole disposition was right out of Hollywood. He always had a sarcastic remark that would just make me laugh.

"Are you up for it, Mike? You won't drop me, will you? said Franklin with a concerned look.

"No way, chief. It's the workout I needed," said Mike.

Soon afterward, Mike and another agent cradled their hands, and Franklin sat as if he were on a chair. They proceeded to bring him up to the top of the tower. Another agent brought up Franklin's wheelchair. I was the last one to go up the steps. I was out of breath when I reached the top. Mike was not breathing heavily at all. He took out one of his cigarettes and took in the view. I have to say it was one of the most beautiful scenes I have ever witnessed. The reds, greens, and blues shined like jewels. Everyone was silent; it was just what we needed; time to reflect.

We were ready to leave the next day. Our plane was prepared to go. Winston had wanted to see us off, but he had a little too much to drink the night before. As our car was getting ready to leave, here came

Winston, running in his bathrobe. Everyone started to laugh. The photographers wanted that picture.

Winston said, "Please, n. Who would want to see me like this?"

The photographers lowered their cameras, and we said our goodbyes. Franklin had a smile on his face and just shook his head.

Chapter 20

A Movie Star - April 20, 1943

As First Dog, I never thought I would be the center of attention and curiosity.

Margaret ran up to me excitedly and said, "Fala, you are going to make a movie."

I could not imagine what this was supposed to be. As First Dog, I was a team player. If it was ok with Franklin, then it's ok with me. The public became fascinated with me. I got many letters from adults, kids, and dogs. Some dogs offered their hand in marriage, some people just wrote about their problems. One guy wrote and told the President how to train me, as if I needed training! Another letter said I needed a haircut. I could not understand why, but Franklin always said my hair gave me personality. I did not need to cut my hair, so I looked like a show dog. No wonder why they wanted to make a movie about me.

Margaret got a letter from MGM saying a movie crew would soon film me at the White House. The guy from MGM said just have Fala do the ole dog tricks. We will provide the narrative. The film's name will be "Fala the President's Dog."

The crew and the cameras were set up in front of the White House lawn. They were reporters there watching while I was being filmed. I used my charm and handled the press very well. I learned everything by watching the Boss with the media. It was easy; all I had to do was listen and look cute. We had a take where I was with Franklin, who gave me commands, begging for food, performing tricks, and listening. I never knew acting was that easy,

We started filming at 7:00 pm, my super time. I did some tricks for food, then went to see Diana Hopkins. We looked at a scrapbook with pictures of me with Winston Churchill; I then ran around the White House lawn and met the press.

The press was always there in one form or another. The reporters would ask me questions, and I would bark and respond to commands. The film was short and was filmed in black and white. When Franklin and I watched it together, I had never heard him laugh so hard.

Then came the cartoons in various newspapers came. Some had me getting thrown out of meetings, questioning things, and my relationships with other dogs. The Boss always got a kick out of the cartoons. Many times he would sit back and shake his head.

I liked the press, and they were very respectful to Franklin. Sometimes, the press could overstep their bounds, but Franklin knew how to handle them. For me, I would just wag my tail.

Chapter 21

Everyone got on Board! - May 20, 1943

The great spirit of the American People showed during these turbulent times. Everyone from all walks of life contributed to the war effort. One group that I was impressed by was the Tuskegee Airmen.

During World War II, racist laws were widespread throughout the country. There were laws mainly in the south that prohibited any form of integration between black and white people. I could never understand this.

During World War I, it was believed by most people in government that black soldiers did not have the ambition and or the ability to operate complicated machinery, let alone fly airplanes.

Eleanor was on the phone with the War Department when I walked into the room when I heard this story. I can tell you my recollections.

During one of her visits in 1941, Eleanor was introduced to Charles Alfred Anderson. He was America's first black pilot. Mr. Anderson was not allowed to go to school, so he taught himself how to fly. At the Tuskegee Institute, Mr. Anderson held classes and taught young black men to be pilots.

Eleanor was very interested in his program for the possible recruitment of soldiers. She felt this program gave black men their place in society which they highly deserved.

After speaking to Mr. Anderson, she asked for a ride in an airplane with him as the pilot.

Being humble, Mr. Anderson said, "Are you sure?"

Eleanor replied, "You would be fine."

She asked for a picture to be taken with Mr. Anderson inside the airplane. You can say a picture says a thousand words!

When Eleanor got home, I followed her into Franklin's office, and she started a conversation with the President about having black pilots in our armed services. FDR agreed. The President had to deal with the complex problem of racism, yet he needed a good working relationship with Congress for the war effort. The Southern part of the United States, which was predominately Republican, gave the President problems since the beginning of his presidency. He had to walk on a tightrope. Eleanor fought; the President compromised. He always said it was politics. Even though it might have been politics, we have to do what is good for the country.

The President successfully ended all discriminatory practices in the armed services that would harm the war effort. He started the Fair Employment Practice Commission, which would oversee that all in the armed services would be treated fairly. The President wanted to push further to integrate the armed services, but the southern part of the United States would not have it.

Soon afterward, an airfield was constructed at the Tuskegee Institute. Training for young black pilots began, and The Tuskegee Airmen were born. Programs in mechanics, aircraft marshaling, and piloting were taught at the college. The Tuskegee airmen were given two planes, the P47 Thunderbolt and the P51 Mustang. Each aircraft had one thing in common; they all had red paint on the planes' tails. Thus, they were called The Red Tails.

These young pilots were under a tremendous amount of pressure to prove they were worthy. If they failed, the racists would win. Nevertheless, the Tuskegee Airmen flew 1,500 missions and earned 95 flying crosses, 14 bronze stars, and 744 Air Medals. They did their job; they did it well. They proved that they were more than worthy of being pilots for the United States of America. I was so proud of these young brave men!

Eleanor was the champion of civil rights! She was disturbed by racial inequality in our country. I overheard many conversations with various Governors, Senators, and Congressmen who represented the southern part of the United States. Many conversations were heated arguments, and I know many people disliked Eleanor for her stance on civil rights. She was committed to civil rights for all people. Her activism brought on a new era for women and defined a new role for the First Lady of The United States.

I was in the war room listening to a few Generals talk about some intelligence that came in. All the intelligence was written in a secret language that had to be decoded. I soon found out the language used was from the Navajo Nation. The American Code Talkers were another group who contributed to the war effort. They were communication specialists that were of Native American descent. These soldiers were responsible for sending coded messages about troop movement and enemy positions. All reports, findings, and transmissions were spoken or written in their Native American languages. All the intelligence would then be reported to their commanding officers. Different tribes of Native Americans participated. The Marines recruited the Navaho Nation in 1941. They started a code-talking school that had four hundred indigenous Navahos. This school became so popular that many of the recruits who joined were under-aged. The code talkers were assigned to fight Japan, North Africa, and Europe. The enemy was not aware of their Native languages, and their work and determination were a vital asset to the intelligence of the United States.

Eleanor was also responsible for getting women out of the house and helping with the war effort. She made many trips to Great Britain, where she observed women serving their country at home and abroad. A letter was placed in the President's basket for a meeting. I went to the Oval Office and overheard a conversation about women serving their country. She told Franklin there were many things women could do and everyone should pitch in.

Not too long after, women were trained by companies such as Ford as mechanics to build aircraft and ships. These workers were referred to as "Rosie the Riveter" were featured in popular magazines all over the country.

Franklin started making some phone calls, and soon afterward, the Woman's Auxiliary Army Corps was established. These women had full military status and were known as WACS. They worked in 300 or more non-combat jobs. The women's Air Force Service Pilots, known as the WASPS, were the first to fly as military combat pilots.

The people of the United States were determined to work hard to win the war. The President was able to think creatively and use all our resources for the war effort. It was brilliant. It allowed people to get involved and allowed everyone to show their abilities and unique talents as a united front against tyranny.

Chapter 22

A Victory Garden - June 7, 1943

Franklin always liked having his closest advisors around when he needed them. He invited Harry Hopkins along with his daughter Diana to live with us at the White House.

Diana would play with me all the time. We would play hide and seek, run around the White House lawn and play fetch with either a branch or a ball. The one thing she loved to do was to hide in the dumbwaiter until Mrs. Nesbit would find her. She would get scolded and sent to her room. One time Diana did not want to see Mrs. Nesbit, so she made a sign that said, "measles, keep out."

Well, this scared the wits out of Mrs. Nesbit. She told poor Diana to meet with the President to discuss her behavior in a stern voice.

"I hear that you and Mrs. Nesbitt are not getting along"' said Franklin with an underlying smile on his face. "I need you to do me a favor. Your father and I have been discussing the idea of having a White House Victory Garden. I want you to oversee the garden. We will grow our vegetables right here at the White House. I want every piece of vacant land in the United States to have a garden. All the food would go to feed the soldiers and the people of the United States!"

Diana agreed and asked, "Can Fala help me with the garden?"

"By all means!" said the President excitedly.

We started the Victory Garden, and I learned how to plant seeds of all different vegetables. We learned to water and weed the ground when it was necessary. My job was to chase the rabbits out of the garden so they did not eat up all our hard work.

Franklin came outside to see the garden and invited the press. Our pictures were all over the newspapers! We were becoming celebrities with our new victory garden!

We grew peppers, tomatoes, carrots, and corn. The colors were so beautiful throughout the yard. When the vegetables were ready, we picked them and brought them to the kitchen.

In the back of my mind, I knew Mrs. Nesbit would find a way to make all of our hard work go down the drain when she cooked the vegetables. I wonder if Franklin was thinking the same thing.

Chapter 23

Another Day Another Conference - August 25, 1943

It was a beautiful hot day in Hyde Park. Word came through once again that Mr. Churchill was coming to visit. Franklin. We just returned from Mexico doing inspections and stayed with President Camacho.

Eleanor came running down the steps, quite upset.

"Franklin, why did you not tell me Mr. Churchill was coming? I am due to leave to visit the troops in the Pacific. I am trying to pack while making arrangements."

Both Franklin and Eleanor had a lot in common, but communication was one of their faults.

"I am sorry, my dear, but I am off to another conference in Quebec, Canada. Winston is coming to get a few days to relax, and then he will leave for Quebec. I will go to Washington first then meet up with Mr. Churchill at Hyde Park before heading to Quebec. Would you like to come with me? I am being pulled in many directions at the same time. I promise to consult with you first in the future," said a besieged President.

"It's no problem dear. I accept your invitation and will develop a better way to communicate," said Eleanor.

She then decided to put a basket at the side of his bed with notes and letters. I know she felt this would help with their communication issues.

Eleanor changed her schedule and arranged to have a picnic on the lawn. Hamburgers, hot dogs, watermelon, all the food I just love. Winston brought his daughter Mary with him. She looked at the food like it came from another planet. I am not sure if she ever had eaten a hot dog and certainly not watermelon.

"Mary, please do not eat the watermelon pits; you don't want them to grow in your stomach." Said Franklin with a straight face.

Everyone laughed and enjoyed the beautiful day. Mary looked bewildered.

If you are not used to the Hudson Valley heat, it can take a toll on you. Mr. Churchill took a walk to the Hudson River and sat down to collect his thoughts for the upcoming meeting. He put his feet in the water and swished them around. Soon it would be time for him to leave for Quebec.

The next day Franklin and I boarded the train, and we were set to go. The idea of staying in a crate was still with me. Now, as First Dog, I had the run of the whole car. Every couple of hours, we had to stop the train so I could relieve myself. Mike Early would take me out. The press always knew when the President was on the train when the "informer" went for a bathroom break.

The name of this meeting was called the Quebec Conference, but the code name was Quadrant. We stayed at the Citadel with the Prime Minister of Canada. It was like living in a castle. I felt like a king!

The purpose of this conference was to discuss the cross-channel invasion of France. The operation was not easy.

Like the North African operation, getting all the equipment across the channel was very difficult, plus this would be a much larger invasion. The allies had to figure out where they would land in France.

While all this talk was going on, Mr. Stalin wrote a cable saying he felt left out and should have been part of the conference. He said he felt like a third wheel, and the allies had not consulted him on any planning. Both Franklin and Winston were furious. These are our troops; we will decide how we use them!

Another subject discussed that would impact world history would be the atomic bomb. Research plans would be underway, but usage rules had to be determined. Both the United States and Great Britain agreed to share research and never use this bomb against each other. The bomb would not be used unless the United States and Great Britain had agreed to it.

Good news from General Eisenhower! The invasion of Sicily was successful! Finally, our troops were ready to invade the Italian mainland.

Franklin snapped his fingers and said, "By George, we are on our way to victory!"

Chapter 24

Cairo, Tehran, Then Back Home - December 10, 1943

I was in the car with Franklin traveling up the mountain to get to Top Cottage. We were scheduled for another hot dog picnic and, more importantly, the chance for me to be a dog again. I miss chasing squirrels and rabbits.

We got good news from the war department! Our boys, led by Generals Patton and Montgomery, landed on the Italian mainland! The Italian government surrendered; however, the Germans fought hard and would not give up.

As Franklin rocked back and forth in his rocking chair, he smiled and said, "One down, two more to go."

Another cable came in, and I saw the look of delight on the President's face. Mr. Stalin had agreed to meet with the Boss and Mr. Churchill for a conference in Tehran, Iran.

The President knew that Marshall Stalin would press him to conduct the cross-channel invasion of France.

The British Prime Minister was very reluctant to the cross-channel invasion for fear that European civilization would be wiped out. Franklin had to put his thinking cap on to try to convince him. So once again, the bags were packed. I got in the car, and I overheard Franklin and Eleanor arguing.

"I'm sorry, no women allowed," he said sternly to Eleanor.

I have to say she was very upset about Franklin's attitude. I never heard him speak like this before. I started to wonder what was going on. The other car pulled up, and Franklin's sons Elliot, FDR JR., and his son-in-law John jumped in.

I felt terrible for Eleanor. She would have made a great advisor on this trip. I think that Franklin had something up his sleeve. Maybe he did not want any distractions. We boarded the Potomac, which took us up to the battleship Iowa. We were on our way to Egypt.

One thing I can tell you about Franklin, he hated to fly. It bothered his sinuses and made him ill. So, going on a battleship on the high seas was a much better option for him. On the other hand, Franklin made good use of his time. He made sure that he played fetch and had me perform tricks in front of the Officers. Franklin read detective stories, brought a few good movies, and went fishing. He was thrilled there were no newspapers.

We were nine days at sea when the battleship pulled into the port of Oran, Algeria. We met with General Eisenhower, who suggested we board a flight from Tunis to Cairo for security reasons. We boarded the plane, much to Franklin's dismay. His attitude changed when he saw the Pyramids, the Sphinx, and the Nile River. What a sight it was!

We landed in Cairo to meet Mr. Churchill and his daughter Sarah. Also, Chaing Kai-Shek, the Chairman from China, with his wife, Madame Chiang, was there. I thought Eleanor would be furious that Madam Chiang was invited and she was not. I am sure Franklin had the same thoughts.

I know the President was very eager to meet Mr. Stalin. The Boss knew he had to use every bit of his political genius to keep the Soviet Union from making a separate peace with Germany.

Dinner was served, and dancing commenced soon afterward. Mr. Stalin approached Franklin with a huge smile on his face. He was small in stature but large in presence.

"I'm so glad to see you, Joseph! It is about time! said the President jokingly." First, Mr. Stalin smiled, then he laughed.

I was given my dinner in the usual place under the table.

As the others sat around the table with their drinks, they discussed the possible subjects addressed the next day. After dinner, Mr. Churchill invited Franklin to his suite for a nightcap. The President declined for fear of getting Mr.Stalin jealous.

Marshal Stalin invited us to the Russian embassy for a tour. We met with the Soviet Generals and had a few drinks.

Franklin found the atmosphere cold and uninviting. The President called Winston and told him about his visit.

He said, "We have to find a way to get Mr. Stalin to trust us. So please do not get angry at what I am about to do."

We were shown to the table by several Soviet Generals; Franklin privately talked with Mr. Stalin. Winston sat there with a confused look on his face. He asked the President what was wrong with Churchill.

The President replied, "Don't worry. He is cranky in the morning."

Franklin started to tease Winston about his drinking and his cigars to Mr. Stalin. I could see the annoyed look coming over Churchill's face. Then, suddenly, Marshall Stalin started teasing Winston also. He did not say a word. He just sat there and took it all in. I am sure if Eleanor had seen this, she would have been furious!

I think Mr. Churchill knew that he would not be able to win his position against the invasion of France. I am sure Franklin was trying to win over the Soviet Union. They all agreed that once Germany was defeated, all would focus on the defeat of Japan.

Mr. Stalin stood up for a toast. "My friends, I am glad we came to this agreement. The most important thing America has done is to help supply us with machines. Without these, we would lose the war."

When all the festivities ended, the President said, "We have proved here that our nations can come together. Even though we have different philosophies of life and different ways of doing things, we can come together for the good of ourselves and the world."

The following day we left for Cairo to continue talks with Mr. Churchill. The plans for the cross-channel invasion were to be set. The first question was who would oversee the attack. Should it be a British or an American General? I knew we were going to need someone really good. This invasion would be more significant than the invasion of North

Africa. During the talks, it was suggested by the Joint Chiefs that General George Marshall should take the lead. George Marshall. I think the President wanted General Marshall to be nearby in Washington.

"Why not Eisenhower?" said the President. "He did a phenomenal job in North Africa. I have full confidence he is the man."

We met General Eisenhower when we got to Tunis, Tunisia.

The President said sternly, "You are one of my most trusted Generals. You are commanding the invasion of France. We will call it Operation Overlord."

Chapter 25

General Patton, Operation Fortitude and D-day - March 15, 1943

During the invasion of Sicily, General Patton was visiting a field hospital. He noticed a soldier who was not physically injured sitting on a bed. The General asked the doctor what was wrong with him. The attending doctor said he suffered from battle fatigue. The General became enraged and started screaming and cursing in the hospital. Patton did not believe battle fatigue existed. He felt the soldier was a coward and proceeded to slap him.

I was in the Oval Office with the President when we found out about this incident. The Boss was very upset about this. He called General Eisenhower and for a meeting to discuss this matter. The President told Eisenhower to order Patton to apologize to the soldier and all he served.

Congress was very upset. When word hit the newspapers about this incident, pressure mounted to remove General Patton. Just another situation on top of many others that aggravated Franklin.

We knew firing Patton was not such a great idea for the war. He knew he was a fierce warrior and would be needed for later engagements. Eisenhower also knew the Nazis admired Patton. With the upcoming invasion of occupied France, he intended to put himself to good use.

Discussions were taking place in the Oval Office on proceeding with the invasion. The allied command decided the area that would be the epicenter of the invasion would be Normandy. They wanted to fool Hitler into believing the attack would be at the Pas de Calais. The Pas de Calais was the shortest distance from Great Britain's mainland to the coast of France, which perfect sense. But how could they fool Hitler?

The first thing the Allies did was send out faulty intelligence to Germany. Two double agents named Mutt and Jeff relayed incorrect messages that the United States sent troops to Scotland. I thought the names were quite comical.

Then another divisive plan was to invade Norway. Soon afterward, Germany sent troops to Norway. Then they fabricated radio transmissions about how to use tanks in extreme cold. We tried our best to confuse Hitler and his Generals so their troops would set up far away from Normandy.

All along the European seaboard, the Germans had fortifications called the Atlantic Wall. If the Allies could spread out the German forces, they would have less power at any one spot. The name of this operation would be called Operation Fortitude.

In a conference with General Marshall, the President decided to put Patton to good use. These discussions lasted through the night.

The President jokingly said, "If anyone could pull this off, it would be George!

General Patton was called to pull off one of the greatest deceptions in military history. Patton was ordered to create a dummy army. German spy planes were flying over Southwest England and saw a massive build-up of tanks and landing craft. German intelligence showed the invasion point would be at the Pas De Calais. The Germans saw tanks, but little did they know they were inflatable. Fake landing craft, airfields, and decoy lighting were also used. The allies also had dummy paratroopers for their false invasion. They would also use tin foil to obstruct enemy radar.

It was brilliant, and it worked. Hitler's generals all told him that Normandy would be the invasion point. It was the weakest part of France, and it was an ideal place to land.

Hitler would not listen and sent troops to Pas de Calais.

Meanwhile, back in Washington, the allies were preparing for the most significant invasion in world history. Operation Overlord consisted of 1200 warships, 400 land craft, and 160,000 allied troops. The uncertainty in the White House if the attack would happen

The weather was not cooperating with the Allies. Every time the Generals thought the attack should be launched, the weather would deteriorate, and the invasion would be called off.

According to the army meteorologists, on June 6, 1944, there would be a small window of better weather. General Eisenhower read the report and gave the order to proceed.

Normandy coastline was a 50-mile stretch. The allies landed on Utah, Omaha, Gold, Juno, and Sword beaches. We sat in the White House; no one spoke a word. We knew many men would be killed in this action. Everyone was silent as Franklin prepared his speech. Finally, word

came in the first wave had landed. We were happy yet sad at the same time. Soon it became time for the President to give a speech to inform the American people about the invasion. The address was in the form of a prayer. He asked for God's blessing for the troops and to give them strength. He said that some of our boys might not make it. He asked God to embrace them and welcome them into his kingdom. The President asked God to give us faith. Operation Overlord was a significant turning point in the war in favor of the Allies. Operation Overload would be a success!

Chapter 26

FDR's Health - February 6, 1944

After the Tehran Conference, I noticed that Franklin had lost weight. In addition, he had a terrible cough, stomach, and sinus problems. The President's Doctor was Admiral Ross McIntyre, who instructed Franklin to have a complete physical at Bethesda Naval Hospital.

While the Doctor was reading the results, the President put his head down and did not say anything. The findings were not promising. The President had hypertension, hypertensive heart disease, and congestive heart failure.

These findings were severe and might influence his decision to run for a 4th term.

The Doctor suggested that he have bed rest for several weeks. He was to have a light diet, very few spices, and no salt. I knew he would not be happy with this. The Doctor prescribed medication for sleeping if needed and codeine for his cough. Franklin's activities were curtailed. He worked from his bed in the morning and had a few hours in the office afternoon. He had limited social activities. He was to rest for 1 hour after each meal. He could not swim in the White House pool. It seemed like all the joy in life was being taken from him.

Even though he had his limitations, he was able to direct the war from his bed. He was able to confer with Generals and Mr. Churchill.

"I want the fourth term! I have to see the beginning of the United Nations! We have to make sure the Soviet Union will join up with our fight against Japan!" said the President.

He was always cheerful and never complained about his health through all of this. He never asked why his cardiologist was checking him two times a day. It was interesting that Franklin always took an interest in his health when he was first diagnosed with polio. He corresponded with his doctors and created and researched new treatments for his condition. It confused me why he was so aloof about his health now.

The war was far from over. Many people close to Franklin felt that he should retire and watch the war conclude. We have a few more trips coming, and I hope all will be well.

Chapter 27

Election, Trip to Alaska, and the Aleutian Islands - August 31, 1944

It was a hot July day when Franklin announced that he would be running for an unheard-of 4th term.

He was determined to stay on to see the future of our country. His dream of the United Nations and Germany and Japan's defeat kept his spirits going.

"All that is within me cries out to go back to my home on the Hudson River," he said.

Eleanor heard about his acceptance for the nomination through talk around the White House.

"Franklin, why is it I am always the last to know everything? It is embarrassing that I have to read or hear such big news from the newspapers or the gossip in the White House!" she said.

She had mixed emotions about how she felt about the fourth term. The war drained Franklin and was affecting his health. Yet, she wanted to see the United Nations' fruition and the social programs she had worked so hard for years ago.

We were off on another trip to Hawaii to discuss the Pacific war, then to Alaska and Aleutian Islands for inspections. There were whispers in Republican circles that The President was not well and would never survive the 4th term.

We boarded the train to California, and we took our time traveling. I loved hearing the conversations between Eleanor and Franklin. It was so nice to see them relax and just enjoy each other's company.

"When this is all over, I want to buy property in the Sahara and teach people how to use irrigation. I would love to teach them about electricity, how to grow crops, you know, to do some good after this whole thing is over." Franklin said,"

"How would we get there by boat? I don't think so. I know how much you hate to fly," said Eleanor with a smile on her face.

It seemed the train ride was taking forever, and Eleanor was starting to get restless, but Franklin was enjoying every minute. The scenery was so beautiful, especially when we were near the Rocky Mountains. I loved sitting on Franklin's lap, looking out the window, and giving a few kisses, of course.

When we were near San Diego, I noticed that Franklin had turned pale.

"I have horrible stomach pains; I guess I ate too fast. Don't call the doctor; I will be fine. I just have to stretch out on the floor."

Franklin was on his back, lying on the floor of the railroad car. Soon after, the pain subsided, and the color was back on his face.

"See, I told you so. I am better; no need for the doctor." Franklin insisted.

He sat up, got into his chair, and I jumped on his lap. I knew something was wrong. I was not quite sure what it was, but something was wrong.

When we got off the train, hundreds of photographers waited for us. It just happened that one photographer took a picture that was not complimentary. Franklin looked exhausted, and his eyes were glassy.

Every person against the President had something to say about that photograph. Roosevelt could not handle the Presidency! He is too ill for the job! My heart sank. I felt terrible for him.

We got on a ship and started sailing to Hawaii to meet up with Generals Nimitz and MacArthur to discuss the Pacific War. We inspected the shipyards, training grounds, and hospitals. Franklin asked one of the secret service guys to wheel him through the hospital's wards to visit the wounded soldiers. He especially wanted to visit those soldiers who had amputations. The Boss wanted to share with them his disability and discuss their bitterness about having useless legs. He smiled at each one. Franklin understood their pain. He wanted them to understand that life was not over, and many great things could be achieved. As we left the hospital, Franklin had tears in his eyes. The war was hitting home.

We were on our way to Alaska when a radiogram came in that Missy had suffered a stroke and died at Chelsea Naval Hospital. She was so young at 46 years old. Missy's death shook Franklin. She was his right-hand girl for many years.

We boarded a large ship, and soon afterward, Franklin delivered a speech. He started to have chest pains with difficulty standing. The ship was rocking back and forth, which did not help. He had lost so much weight his braces did not fit properly. When we got to the Captain's quarters, he fell into the chair. The President's staff called the doctor into Franklin's quarters, and a cardiogram was performed. He also had blood work done, and the doctor advised him to rest.

I was sitting on the deck, and many sailors came up to me to pat me on the head. Then, one sailor got the idea to take a piece of my fur and cut it off with a pair of scissors. Soon everyone wanted a piece. When they were all finished, I was a bald dog! I walked back to Franklin's cabin, and he had a shocked look on his face.

"Fala, what did they do to you?"

I could tell Franklin was agitated. Finally, he told the ship's Captain to say to his Sailors that any form of affection to Fala should be in the form of a pat on the head.

We had dinner with General MacArthur and General Nimitz to discuss the war in the Pacific. There was a massive map on the wall, and the Generals were explaining their positions and strategies. They all came to a joint agreement. After that, we left for the Aleutian Islands for another inspection. Finally, we returned home and started to get ready for the campaign.

Chapter 28

Quebec Conference and the Fala Speech - September 30, 1944

Once again, we were off to Quebec to meet with Winston Churchill to discuss the war and its conclusion. Eleanor joined us, which was a good thing, especially after the debacle of the Tehran Conference.

Franklin was the first to arrive. Mr. Churchill walked up to him and shook his hand. Winston was his usual self, gave his greeting, and wanted to get inside to discuss the war over his brandy and cigars.

Eleanor said to Franklin," I think he likes me, but I think he feels women should be seen and not heard."

Clementine Churchill was there also. The girls' visit included shopping and a trip to the countryside. They would also sit for tea and do social meetings with other women. I know Eleanor would have rather been in the trenches with the men discussing the war.

Through much debate, Roosevelt and Churchill agreed that Germany's war industries would be replaced by farming and pastoral production. The next step was to discuss the Pacific. Mr. Churchill stated that Great Brittan stood with the United States against the Empire of Japan. The President was delighted that our greatest ally was with us. The final blow would be Japan's invasion, which would only happen after Germany's defeat.

After dinner, I noticed Winston talking to Franklin's Doctor. He was worried about the President's health. Dr. McIntire assured the Prime Minister the President was just fine.

Winston said," We cannot afford to lose that man."

Later on, that evening, Dr. McIntire decided to take the President's blood pressure. The Doctor's recorded it 240/130. Not good; not good at all.

We left Quebec and went back to Hyde Park for a much-needed rest. Winston joined us there also. He loved Hyde Park. He loved sitting on the lawn, having picnics, drinking his brandy, and enjoying a good talk. Unfortunately, Winston's habits of staying up until the wee hours of the morning were not good for the Boss' health. Franklin needed his rest, and soon after, Mr. Churchill left Hyde Park and went back to England.

Franklin said, "Don't wake me up; I want to sleep the whole night through and well into the morning."

We returned to Washington later in the week, and the President was preparing for a speech to the Teamsters Union. The Meeting was taking place with his campaign managers when I heard,

"Oh, that's ridiculous! Are they desperate for stories?" said President Franklin, who quickly got his pen and paper to address this story. I listened to the radio, and I could not believe my ears. The Republicans accused the President of turning a battleship back to the Aleutian Islands because I was missing. The taxpayers had to foot the bill. They continued to say the President abused his powers.

At the Teamsters meeting with that Roosevelt charm, he spoke about the incident and how the Republicans made up such a ridiculous story.

He said, "I am accustomed to hearing malicious falsehoods about myself, but I think I have the right to resent, to object to a libelous statement about my dog."

He proceeded to say that my Scotch soul was furious! Which it was! The crowd erupted in laughter. The speech was a great success. Historians have said this speech was the glue that sealed the election's fate and gave the President an unprecedented 4th term.

I can tell you I was never left behind on the island, and the President never sent back a destroyer to retrieve me. It was all fabrication and political nonsense. Franklin knew how to use these attacks and make them turn in his favor. That is what was so magical about Franklin. His wit and charm would win him an unprecedented fourth term.

Chapter 29

Campaigning and Election Day – October 21, 1944

I want to talk about Election Day. While rumors were floating around about me and the nonsense about the Aleutian Islands, there was also a terrible rumor that Franklin had suffered a stroke and had a heart attack.

Rumors about a secret operation for cancer and he needed around-the-clock care from a nurse were all around Washington.

We left for New York to campaign and took a tour of Manhattan, Brooklyn, The Bronx, and Queens. We would see a lot of people that day. In the afternoon, it started to rain. The streets were flooded, and it was frigid.

The doctor recommended that Franklin say inside the car and wave to the people through the windows. The President would not have it.

"I want the people to see that I am alive," he said.

It rained so hard that we were all drenched. The rain was all over Franklin's face, glasses, and clothes. Finally, we arrived at Ebbets Field, where a huge crowd was waiting for us.

Franklin was able to get up and walk to the podium and tell the crowd that he was always a Dodgers Fan. He promised to come back and watch the Dodgers win. He smiled and waved. His charm warmed the crowd, and their applause was deafening.

We traveled to Boston and went to Fenway Park. The crowds greeted us with overwhelming applause. The crowd was excited to see us, then headed to Hyde Park to hear the election results.

We had several guests at Springwood, and there was a nervousness in the air as the Roosevelt staff served the guests cider and donuts. By

10:00 that evening, we knew the election results. The President won 53.5% of the popular vote and 432 electoral votes. I was happy we won, but I knew that I knew Franklin was not well in the back of my mind.

In the usual fashion, when The President won the election, he put on his wool cape and walked to the front porch to greet the people of Hyde Park. It was their torchlight parade, a tradition after a Roosevelt win. He smiled and waved to the crowd. Then, he invited the reporters inside for refreshments and good conversation.

Chapter 30

Buttons - January 2, 1945

Franklin had a very good friend named Hendrich Van Loon.

Mr. Van Loon had a dog named Noodle who always accompanied him. I always cracked up at his name. Noodle Van Loon. I know Franklin never wanted to insult Mr. Van loon, so he kept very quiet. I know deep down inside he was laughing up a storm.

Noodle and I quickly became friends. We would have great times running around the White House, stealing table scraps, playing with any children we could find, and of course chasing squirrels.

Around 1943, Margaret introduced me to a Scottie named Buttons. She was very small for her breed. She would never come over to us. She always would stay with Margaret usually under her feet.

One day Noodle told me he overheard the President say he wanted me to have a family to "continue the line." I thought to myself shouldn't I have a say in the matter?

I get letters every day from females that want to meet me. Some were Scotties; some were not. I do have to admit that some of the girls were quite pretty. All were well groomed, putting their best paw forward. Many had bows in their hair, sometimes sitting on their front porch or had portraits taken by a local photographer. Many letters were received asking for my hand in marriage. I always saw the staff putting all these pictures in a folder. I really could not understand why they kept each piece of mail I received.

Margaret brought Buttons over to the White House. As I entered the room, Button saw me and ran way under the table. Noodle was sitting there trying to play matchmaker, but Buttons would not have it. So, I thought I would go over to her to say hello. Buttons growled at me and bit my ear. I could hear Noodle in the background laughing.

For some reason, Buttons did not like me. and I am not sure why.

Many years later, Buttons came over and still never forgot how to bark, growl, and bite me. If Franklin thinks this is going to work, he is nuts.

I had not seen Noodle for a while, and there was no one around who could advise me. I was tired of her coming to my house, eating my food, and biting me. I know Franklin would love for us to have puppies, but I am not sure what to do.

Margaret made an appointment at the Vet. I thought maybe they might have a solution. A few weeks later, through the genius of medical science, Buttons was pregnant! You would think she would be receptive towards me. I guess I was asking too much. She still disliked me and tried to bite me every time I saw her.

While I was at the vet, the press was interested in where I was. Eleanor stated in her my day column that I was getting married and that a honeymoon would be soon after. Many people wrote letters saying that marriage was a sacred institution that should not involve anything other than a human. I could not believe what I was hearing. I do not think Eleanor gave it a second thought.

Soon afterwards Buttons gave birth to 2 beautiful female black Scotties. I was the father of Twins! Franklin came up to me when the birth announcement came and petted me on the head.

"You did a good job, ole boy."

Franklin named my daughters Meggie and Peggie.

One afternoon the President asked if I wanted to go for a ride. I knew we were going to Wilderstein.

As I exited the car, I ran to the house and saw Buttons with my daughters. They were perfect! I went over to their pen and started to play with them. Buttons waited in the corner, giving me dirty looks.

The pups were eager to play. I showed them how to chase squirrels and do tricks. The most important thing I wanted to teach them was how not to get lost.

As the President and I were leaving, I looked over at Buttons and wanted to thank her for being a great mother to Meggie and Peggie. She looked at me and barked. I guess it was her way of saying all was well.

Chapter 31

The Election and Inauguration Day - January 20, 1945

Election day came and went. I was not surprised the President won a fourth term. I felt deep in his heart he wanted to retire. We were winning the war, yet news from Eastern Europe was getting worse by the day. The information about the concentration camps and people without homes or food in Europe and Japan was overwhelming. The Nazis were on the run, but Japan was fighting harder than ever.

The whole Roosevelt family descended onto the White House to celebrate the Inauguration. All the rooms were loaded with men, women, and children. It was Franklin's wish to have the whole family together. He wanted the feeling of family. He tried to laugh with the kids and talk to his sons and daughter about good times.

After the Inauguration, there would be a luncheon for about 2000 guests. In the morning, Franklin was reading the New York Times. He threw the paper down onto his lap and called for Eleanor.

"That woman just never knows when to stop! Here look at this! The headline of the New York Times! Housekeeper Rejects Roosevelt's Menu Choice for Luncheon. I wanted Chicken A LA King. Mrs. Nesbitt refused my request. She said she could not serve a hot meal for 2000 people. My first order for my fourth term is to fire that woman. I think that is the reason why I agreed to a fourth term!"

After the Inauguration, the luncheon began. The President was wheeled into the main dining room when I heard him say to his son.

"James, I am having stabbing chest pain again. Go get me a stiff drink so I can get through this."

There were whispers amongst the guests that said the President looked very ill. Many commented on his weight loss and his gray pallor. To add more stress to the evening, Mrs. Nesbit did not defrost enough chicken, and there was not enough useable chicken for 2000 people. When served, there was hardly any chicken but a lot of celery in the chicken salad. Everyone commented there was a lot of celery. I know Franklin was embarrassed but tried to make the best out of it. Everyone was laughing, but I knew he was fuming.

"Franklin said, "That woman has been killing me for three terms, and now she starts on the fourth!"

Everyone had a great time, and the guests left. Franklin was alone in the Oval Office, deep in thought. I cannot get this image out of my head. He looked so sad. I wonder if he knew the end could be near.

Chapter 32

Yalta - February 5, 1945

We would be meeting with Mr. Churchill and Marshall Stalin at Yalta, a Soviet port on the Black Sea. This trip would be very long, and I wondered if Franklin was physically up to doing this. We would be at sea for over a week. We boarded the USS Quincy in Newport News, Virginia. I was surprised that Franklin's daughter Anna was on board and not Eleanor.

"I just do not want a fuss with reporters and them interfering with our meetings," he said.

We were sitting on the deck enjoying the weather. The President talked about the different species of birds that live along the shoreline. He spoke of life, not about the war. I could tell he missed Lucy. We were sailing by the area she grew up.

"This is where Lucy is from; such a nice area." He said with a smile on his face.

He continued with the conversation about the birds.

It was getting close to Franklin's birthday, and Anna wanted to make sure the day was festive for her father. Cakes were made by Navy cooks representing the four terms as President. One small cake was asking for a fifth term.

Franklin laughed and said, "Let me get through this one."

Lucy and Margaret had sent birthday gifts, and the Navy delivered them. They were the typical presents that Franklin would have loved. He loved gag gifts and little trinkets as mementos. The big hit was a cigarette lighter that could be used when the wind blew.

"Now that was some invention!" he laughed.

We were getting close to the Mediterranean Sea, and the crew told the President that Mr. Churchill would be flying into Malta. We soon arrived in Malta, and Franklin was wheeled to the ship's deck and greeted Mr. Churchill.

Franklin, with a big smile and his cigarette pointing towards the sky, said, "I think we need to end this thing, Winnie!"

Winston replied, "Here Here!"

Later that evening, there was a dinner to celebrate the occasion.

"Thank God Mrs. Nesbit is not here. So, I now can enjoy the food," jokingly said the President.

Anna made sure Franklin was not up all hours with Mr. Churchill. He needed his rest. We would be flying out to Russia before midnight. Franklin was taken to his cabin after several meetings with Mr. Churchill, who then commented to his associate, "My God, he looks so weak. I was shocked. I will keep this to myself. I do not want to stress him out. I want to make this visit as enjoyable as possible."

The plane ride was freezing and bumpy. Upon exiting the plane, we were met by the Russian honor guards. We then got into a car and drove 80 miles to Yalta.

Franklin looked so tired. He was breathing very heavily, and his hands were shaking. He smiled at me and patted my head, and told me things were going to be okay.

The conference took place at the Livadia Palace in Crimea. This palace belonged to Czar Nicholas before the Russian Revolution. It seemed ironic that we met in a palace that belonged to a Czar that Mr. Stalin overthrew.

The building was quite beautiful and located in the mountains. The gilded rooms were decorated with many paintings and sculptures. I loved the courtyard with all the beautiful plants and palm trees. Watching Mr. Churchill walk around in a tall black fur hat was amusing.

At this time in the war, the Soviet Union was closing in on Germany in the east. The Allies were coming in from the West. General

Patton was plowing through western Europe with Willie by his side. I think of Willie often and hope he is okay.

The Allies and their chief of staff sat at a round table discussing Germany's fate and post-war Europe.

The Soviet Union had catastrophic losses during the war. In the meeting, Marshall Stalin stated he wanted satellite countries surrounding Russia as protection. In return, he agreed two weeks after Germany's surrender, Russia would join the allies to defeat Japan.

Winston Churchill wanted a democratic Poland. Poland helped out the British forces during the war and felt a democratic government would be the gift they deserved.

The United States and its allies needed the Soviet Union to help them with the war against Japan. Mr. Stalin knew this and used it as leverage to get what he wanted. Post-war Europe would be divided into sections belonging to each Allied country. Each allied country had terms and conditions that had to be decided upon.

The first was an unconditional surrender. Hitler would be removed from office by the Allied supreme command. All war criminals would be tried and sentenced. Germany would be divided into East Germany and West Germany.

The Soviets would control the East. West Germany would be divided into three sections operated by the United States, Great Britain, and France.

The second condition was to get the Soviet Union to join the United Nations. Roosevelt wanted Russia to be a member of the Security Council of the United Nations.

Mr. Churchill did not get democracy in Poland even though Stalin agreed to elections. Later on, the Soviets arrested those who were setting up the elections, and Poland became Communist.

I noticed a change in Franklin's health. He could just about hold a cup and saucer. He found it challenging to sign his name. He used to shave, and now he needed this valet to shave him. I also noticed a depression in Franklin's demeanor. The doctors removed everything he loved. He was not allowed to swim anymore; he had to cut down on smoking; he had to cut down on his social life. He even asked Eleanor to drive him when he was home.

I feel I am slowly losing my friend. He puts on a real show, but I know how sick he was.

Chapter 33

Meeting with Saudi King Abdul Aziz - February 14, 1945

We left Yalta with many agreements among the Allies. We had to stop by the Suez Canal to meet with King Abdul Aziz of Saudi Arabia on our way home. The USS Murphy would be transporting the King to meet with us.

I was sitting on the deck with Franklin when the ship appeared. The ship looked a little strange from a distance, but we could not believe what we saw when it got closer. The entire deck of the USS Murphy was covered with a beautiful Arabian tent. The guns on the deck were being used as tent poles. The floors were covered with beautifully designed carpets.

"Will you look at that! A sight that we probably will never see again!" said the President in amazement.

On the ship's deck were fresh vegetables, sacks of rice, and several sheep. The quarters on the ship were very small. The captain was unsure where he should put the King. Aziz requested not to sleep in one of the commander's rooms but to sleep in one of his tents. The King also had his bodyguards, astrologer, and coffee servers in attendance.

Mostly everyone associated with the King was sleeping on the deck. I found out later King Aziz was raised in the desert and always lived in a tent. The idea of sleeping around four walls made the King claustrophobic. King Aziz also had the ship's navigator tell him which way was east so they could pray in the direction of the holy city of Mecca. All of this, of course, had to be confirmed by the King's Astrologer.

The King and his entourage, along with the American sailors aboard the USS Quincy, were somehow able to communicate without speaking to each other. I always found it amazing that hand gestures can work as well as spoken language. The sailors showed the King's people their way around the ship, and in return, the sailors were able to examine the clothes and daggers of the Saudi men.

According to rank, the Saudi government gave each American sailor 10-15 pounds of sterling silver. In addition, officers were given a watch with the King's name inscribed, and the Caption of the Quincy received a traditional Arab costume and a gold dagger. In return, the USS Murphy gave King Aziz two submachine guns and a pair of navy binoculars which he fancied.

The King liked American food, but he always had some lamb and rice at the table. Aziz's chef prepared these side dishes. The aroma of various spices throughout the ship made me so hungry. The King was very fond of apples and requested an apple pie a-la-mode. The conversation consisted of humor and King Aziz telling everyone of his battles and hand-to-hand combat. Everyone sat around the King, listening to his stories. I found him to be quite entertaining.

The big meeting was on the deck of the USS Quincy. The conference took about an hour, discussing post-war developments and the United Nations. The King invited us to the USS Murphy for dinner, but we had to decline to keep on schedule. The President was advised that King Aziz would be insulted if an Arabic meal did not accompany their talk. Franklin insisted that a great cup of coffee might do the trick. The King was delighted as he shared a good cup of Arabic coffee with his friend.

Before they left, King Aziz mentioned to Franklin about the war wounds on his legs and how difficult it was to walk around. The King was admiring the President's wheelchair.

"You are luckier than I because you still have your legs. I have to be wheeled around wherever I go", said Franklin

"No, my friend, you are more fortunate.

Your chair will take you wherever you want to go. Unfortunately, my legs are getting weaker by the day," said the King.

"If you like my chair so much, I have an extra onboard. That is my gift to you." smiled the President."

Franklin has such a kind heart. The Saudi King treasured his gift and their newfound friendship.

Chapter 34

The Speech Before Congress and Continued Bad News - March 12, 1945

Upon returning to Washington, Franklin reported to congress the deal made at the Yalta Conference. Franklin was very weak. He was tired and looked very ill. I do not think the public was aware of how ill he was.

There was a big difference in Franklin's appearance, and the whispers were throughout the halls of Congress said he was not well. I think Franklin knew deep in his heart that he needed to address this issue.

For the first time, The President sat down while making a speech. I do not think he could physically stand long enough. He was seated in a regular chair with a table in front of him.

I was sitting in the Oval Office with the Joint Chiefs of Staff when the President started the speech.

When he started, he begged the pardon of Congress because he was seated. He continued to say with 10 pounds of steel around his legs and having completed a 14,000-mile trip. He needed to sit. He also told Congress it was good to be home.

I let out a whimper. The speech made me very sad. That was the first time I could ever remember Franklin admitting his disability in a public forum. The Congress then gave a loud applause.

The President called for the defeat of Germany and the unconditional surrender of Japan. He called for Congress to accept the Charter of the United Nations. The countries would be meeting in San Francisco to start the process.

Franklin wanted to go to Warm Springs to rest and get away from the war. Even though Germany was very close to defeat, some circumstances plagued his mind.

In June 1944, the United States was informed about a concentration camp liberated by the Soviet Union. The reports were unbelievable. Our intelligence was not quite sure if the Soviet reports were accurate. They spoke about inmates starved to death, numerous bodies piled on top of each other, rotting in the sun. The more camps became liberated, the more intelligence about the conditions started to come in. The United States armed forces came upon a concentration camp called Ohrdruf. Both Eisenhower and Patton were requested to come immediately. General Eisenhower was appalled by what he saw. General Patton got physically sick when he saw the conditions of the camp. I know General Patton very well. He was called old blood and guts for being a tough and strong leader. The situation at this concentration camp was something he had never seen before. Many people died in this camp, and the numbers were unbelievable. This situation must have been horrible for a reaction from General Patton. What he saw made him physically ill. A call was made directly to General Marshall to have Congress and Journalists report and witness what they saw at the newly liberated camps. They wanted the world to see the Nazi atrocities and have a first-hand account if people were to say it never happened.

Franklin read the reports and could not believe his eyes. We would never know the numbers of the dead until much later on. Franklin knew the numbers were huge, and it weighed heavily on his mind.

The Nazis killed 11 million civilians. Six million were Jews, and 5 million included people with disabilities, Roma (Gypsies), Jehovah's Witnesses, and Homosexuals. We would find out these camps were actual killing machines for anyone considered enemies of the Nazi State.

The continuing war with Japan also plagued his mind. He knew Japan was going to fight to the very end. Should the United States invade Japan? Would it be a wise decision?

Could we count on Stalin's help after the defeat of Germany?

Many people did not know that Franklin had a secret in his back pocket. It was called The Manhattan Project. We had the most outstanding scientists in the world creating the atomic bomb. The President made sure no one knew about it, not even his Vice President Harry Truman. The only country that knew about the atomic bomb was Great Britain. What we did know was this bomb would kill many people, mostly civilians. It would bring Japan to its knees if the bomb were used.

I am not sure if Franklin would have used the Atomic Bomb. However, the war with Germany was not over, and we were waiting to hear from Marshall Stalin. Once Germany was defeated, hopefully, Russia would keep its word to help the Allies in Japan's defeat.

I was in meetings where all this information was being discussed with President. I could tell it was affecting him not only emotionally but also physically. There were times I could read his mind. I know he felt this was all too much.

His hands were tied until Germany was defeated.

Chapter 35

April 12, 1945

The house was quiet. I was half asleep in my favorite corner at the Little White House in Warm Springs, Georgia. I always loved it there. A lot of open lands to run around and lots of squirrels and rabbits to chase. A dog could quickly get used to living here. I had a comfortable bed and good food, and the smell of the barbecue grill was telling me Franklin was having a party today.

I knew all I had to do was perform a few tricks to get a piece of that delicious food. You know the ole give me your paw and that rollover trick. Even though Franklin instructed his staff not to feed me table scraps, all rules were broken when the party began. I just had to tip my head to the side, lick a few fingers, and give a few kisses, and someone was bound to share a piece of steak or chicken. I could not look overzealous, or the Boss would have figured out my plan.

There were many special guests invited to the house that day. One talented person was with the President in his study. Her name was Elizabeth, whom Franklin commissioned to paint his portrait. I am not sure why Franklin wanted his portrait painted. He was not well recently. His face was pale and thin, and Franklin had recently lost a lot of weight. His face also had a lot of new lines, and he always looked tired. I was not the only one who was concerned about Franklin. Most of our friends from the White House and staff have noticed the same. It was suggested to Franklin by his friends and doctors that a trip to Warm Springs might be the best medicine. It was a quiet place, an excellent place to get away from the war. I thought it was a good idea. Warm Springs always gave us much-needed rest.

I remember the aroma of food was getting more robust, and the guests would be arriving soon. I walked over to the Boss's room to see what was going on to hide my excitement. I did not intend to stay long. I just wanted to know when the party was to begin.

As I entered the room, Elizabeth was painting the portrait and telling ghost stories simultaneously. I looked over to the other side of the room, and Lucy Mercer was sitting on the couch. Lucy was a friend of Franklin's from a long time ago. She looked so beautiful. She was enjoying the storytelling and was laughing. Anna, the President's daughter, and Laura Delano, the President's cousin, also contributed and made the stories scarier. Franklin looked very handsome despite his tired look. The portrait that Elizabeth was painting was quite good. It was amazing how realistic the painting was. I found it interesting how Elizabeth could tell such great stories and paint simultaneously.

I heard the valet enter the room, and he informed everyone it was time to eat. Franklin glanced at his watch.

"Just 15 more minutes please," he said.

He turned around and smiled at Lucy when he started to rub his forehead. Then, he dropped his cigarette on the floor.

"I have a pain in the back of my head and chest."

Within seconds the President collapsed onto the floor. Both Lucy and Elizabeth were shocked and called for help.

While the doctor was on his way, Anna and Laura tried to move Franklin to the nearest bedroom. There were so many people in the room; it was hard to see what was going on. I heard the President trying to breathe. He struggled to breathe and gasped for air. Finally, the doctor came and tried everything in his power to keep Franklin alive.

All of this confusion became overwhelming for me. I needed to get out of the room and out of the house. I ran to the screen door and saw that it was closed. I wanted to get out of the house. I was so desperate I ran to the door as fast as possible to break the screen. First try, nothing; the second try, nothing; on the third try, I was able to break the screen and run free. I ran as fast as I could. I could feel the wind on my face; my heart was beating fast. I ran so quickly that I could not breathe, but I kept running up and down the hills.

I am not sure why, but I stopped abruptly, and I let out a big howl. Then, I screamed at the top of my lungs.

In my heart, I knew the President was now dead.

Chapter 36

Losing my best friend, The Funeral, And A Broken Heart - April 20, 1945

His body was to be brought back to Washington. Eleanor arrived and went straight to the bedroom. She knew Lucy was there. Eleanor was very quiet and requested to be alone with her husband. I often wonder what she said to him. I cannot imagine how she felt.

We boarded the train for Washington along with Franklin's bronze casket. The train started slowly, and the word how gotten out about the President's death. People were lined all along the railroad tracks. Americans were crying, standing on boxes so they could see their fallen leader. All types of people were there. Men, Women, Children, Black and White, all stood together as Americans to say goodbye to their President.

The funeral took place in Washington and another last train ride to Hyde Park. On the way home, I thought to myself; you are home now, my friend; just as you wanted to be.

There were many times I heard a car coming up the driveway. I had to run because I heard that familiar sound to ensure it was not him. It took me a long time to believe he was gone. Every morning I would walk over to his grave.

Possibility to catch his scent, maybe to see his spirit. His presence was still in the house. I could smell his scent on his bed and the furniture. I would walk over to his closet just to see his clothes. It was comforting yet very sad.

Margaret was willing to have me live at Wilderstein with her. She visited to discuss this with Eleanor.

"I will never allow it, Margaret! Fala is part of the family. I will take him with me to Val Kill. He will keep me company and occupied."

After Franklin's death, Eleanor continued her work for the social program she had worked so hard for and continued Franklin's dream of creating the United Nations.

As I breathe the air of Val Kill, I am home, Eleanor is here, and Franklin is in my heart. We will always be together.

Chapter 37

Leadership - June 7, 1945

I was sitting at Val Kill, watching and listening to the water flow over the rocks in the creek near the house. For some reason, the sound has a very calming effect. My thoughts turn to Franklin. I miss his smile, his laugh; I miss his very being.

I could not help but reflect on our life together. However, I had one question I needed to have answered before ending this chapter of my life. What made Franklin Roosevelt a great leader? What made him the person he was?

I did not witness the great depression, but I heard stories about people's helplessness during those times. He cared about the ordinary person. He made a New Deal with the American People, restoring their dignity and belief in the American government. He was a brilliant politician and understood how to work with his opponents to achieve his goals. Many will look upon his policies with discontent, but he was a man of his time and felt his plans were the most important, no matter how he got there.

Franklin gained the American people's trust during World War II by talking to them as a trusted friend. His fireside chats had the nation huddled around their radios. He spoke to the people in a language they could understand. He confronted congress in times of enormous stress and never got too far ahead of his followers. He understood them and kept them informed. He read their mail; he even got a kick out of the letters sent to me. He always kept in tune with the wants and needs of the American people.

He was always thinking outside of the box. He was reshaping, reforming, and putting new programs in place. His thoughts were of the future. How can we make this world better? He had the skill, the knowledge, and the experience to make change happen.

Franklin also showed he could relate to the ordinary person during the war. He inspired his people by using ration books in the White House. He made sure that he should not be eating better than the everyday person because he was the President. When the government asked for women to donate their nylon stockings, Eleanor started wearing black tights to show women an example, and she was one of them. They were both able to inspire others through their ethics and character.

He would always say, "Just because I am in the White House does not mean I am better than the man who serves me my coffee."

Franklin was always ambitious. He was still finding new ways to make himself a better person. When Franklin came down with polio, he became an expert on the disease and opened a rehabilitation center. Then, in true Roosevelt style, he learned to walk and became the United States President. Franklin always emerged stronger as times became tough and insisted that you become a better person when you remember where you came from.

He had the right temperament for the times. He was confident he could get the job done. He was brilliant, creative, and was able to problem-solve.

When I was on the train heading to Washington for Franklin's funeral, all the people along the railroad tracks showed their love for him. People were crying, waving, and showing their emotions. So many did not know any other President. Four terms, 16 years is a very long time.

I had a great life with Franklin. Without him, my world would have been empty. He was my friend, my leader, and my teacher. I am onto another chapter in my life with Eleanor. More life to live, more experiences to have. I will always visit Franklin whenever I can. When I see the long pathway at Springwood, I remember walking to Albany Post Road with him. I remember the conversations and the love of life that

Franklin had.

I know he will be waiting for me at The Rainbow Bridge when it is my time. I will walk with him again; he will have no braces and no limitations. We will discuss what a wonderful life we had.

Epilogue

After President Roosevelt's untimely death in 1945, Fala lived with Eleanor at Val- Kill and had a full life. He was matched with Margaret's Scottie named Buttons and fathered twin girls. They were named Meggie and Peggy. In addition, Fala witnessed the creation of the United Nations, Franklin Roosevelt's dream, with Eleanor by his side.

Fala died in 1952 and is buried alongside the President at Hyde Park, New York.

About the Author

My relationship with Fala started with my first trip to the Franklin Delano Roosevelt Memorial in Washington, D.C. The little dog that was sitting at the President's feet intrigued me.

My interest in World War II came from my mother. Her numerous stories about the war compelled me to read any book I can find. That is when my admiration for President Franklin Roosevelt started.

While in college, in my Master's program in Art Education, I incorporated my love for Art and history and wrote a thesis entitled "Art in the Third Reich."

The Fala project started 25 years ago with numerous trips to The Presidential Library in Hyde Park and speaking with many archivists and Park Rangers at the library, and I was able to put the history of the time using the voice of Fala.

With retirement starting after 21 years of teaching, I was finally able to complete this project.

I currently live in Princeton, New Jersey, and I am starting a new phase of my life.

Bibliography

Axelrod, Alan. Nothing to Fear: Lessons in
Leadership From FDR, Portfolio, 2003

Gallagher, Hugh Gregory. FDR's Splendid Deception,
Vandamere Press, 1994

Jackson, Robert H. That Man An Insider's Portrait of
Franklin Roosevelt, Oxford University Press, 2003

Kearns-Goodwin, Doris. No Ordinary
Time, Touchstone.1994

Klara, Robert. FDR's Funeral Train, Palgrave Macmillan,
2010

Lelyveld, Joseph. His Final Battle; The Last Months of
Franklin Roosevelt, Alfred A. Knopf , 2016

Newton, Verne W. FRD and the Holocaust, St. Martin's
Press, 1996

Robinson, Greg. By Order of the President: FDR and the
Internment of Japanese Americans

Roosevelt, Eleanor. My Day, Pharos Books, 1989

Stafford, David. Roosevelt and Churchill, Men of Secrets,
The Overlook Press, 1999

Suckley, Margaret. Closest Companion: The Unknown
Friendship between Franklin Roosevelt and Margaret
Suckley, Houghton Mifflin Company, 1995

Woolner, Davis B. The Last 100 Days: FDR at War and
Peace, Basic Books, 2017